Optical Character Recognition of Old Manuscripts Using Artificial Intelligence

Thomas Edison

CHAPTER 1

Introduction

1.1 Historical and Cultural Context of Manuscripts in Human Civilization

Manuscripts represent the most fundamental and enduring medium through which human civilizations have preserved, transmitted, and accumulated knowledge across generations. Before the advent of mechanical printing in the 15th century CE, and for many centuries thereafter in regions where printing technology arrived late or remained expensive, manuscripts constituted the exclusive means by which intellectual, spiritual, literary, administrative, and technical knowledge moved through time and space.

1.1.1 Manuscripts as Vessels of Human Knowledge Across Civilizations

The very word "manuscript" derives from the Latin manu scriptum, literally "written by hand," emphasizing the intimate relationship between human craftsmanship and knowledge preservation. The significance of manuscripts extends far beyond their functional role as information storage media. Each manuscript embodies multiple layers of historical meaning: the intellectual content of the text itself; the material culture reflected in substrate selection, preparation techniques, and preservation practices; the paleographic evidence of script evolution and scribal conventions; the social and economic contexts indicated by patronage patterns, institutional custodianship, and commissioning practices; and the aesthetic sensibilities manifested in calligraphic artistry, decorative illumination, and physical design. Manuscripts thus serve as primary sources not merely for the texts they contain but for understanding the societies, technologies, belief systems, and artistic traditions that produced and valued them.

1.1.2 Diversity of Manuscript Traditions Across World Cultures

Human societies across all inhabited continents developed manuscript traditions utilizing locally available organic and inorganic materials adapted to climatic conditions, cultural preferences, and technological capabilities. The diversity of these traditions reflects both universal human needs for knowledge preservation and the particular environmental, cultural, and historical circumstances of different civilizations. In ancient Mesopotamia, clay tablets impressed with cuneiform script dating from circa 3200 BCE represent among the earliest surviving manuscripts, with their durability through millennia contrasting dramatically with the fragility of organic manuscripts. Ancient Egypt employed papyrus scrolls manufactured from the pith of the papyrus plant (Cyperus papyrus) growing abundantly in the Nile Delta, with surviving examples including religious texts such as the Book of the Dead, administrative records, literary works, and scientific treatises spanning from the 4th millennium BCE through the early Islamic period. The Greco-Roman world initially utilized papyrus scrolls inherited from Egyptian technology, later transitioning to parchment codices (bound books with pages) manufactured from prepared animal skins during the early centuries of the Common Era. This format innovation, strongly associated with early Christian communities who found the codex form more practical for liturgical use than unwieldy scrolls, gradually displaced scroll format throughout the Mediterranean world and medieval Europe. Medieval European manuscript culture reached extraordinary heights of artistry in illuminated manuscripts produced in monastic scriptoria, where monks painstakingly copied religious texts, classical literature, and scientific works, often decorating them with gold leaf, mineral pigments, and intricate miniature illustrations that represent masterpieces of medieval art. In East Asia, distinct manuscript traditions emerged utilizing materials and formats adapted to regional conditions. Chinese civilization developed sophisticated manuscript culture initially employing bamboo and wooden slips bound with cords (circa 1500 BCE onward), transitioning to silk manuscripts for prestigious texts, and culminating in paper manuscript technology following the invention of paper during the Han Dynasty (circa 105 CE). The Chinese manuscript tradition profoundly influenced Korean, Japanese, and Vietnamese manuscript cultures through cultural diffusion along trade routes and diplomatic channels. Japanese manuscripts employed paper manufactured from kozo (mulberry) and other plant fibers, with distinctive formats including scrolls (emaki), folded books (orihon), and bound volumes (sasshi) reflecting particular functional and aesthetic preferences. In the Islamic world, manuscript culture flourished from the 7th century CE onward, initially utilizing parchment and papyrus, later transitioning predominantly to paper following its transmission from China through Central Asia. Islamic manuscripts are renowned for extraordinary calligraphic artistry in Arabic script with its multiple regional styles (Kufic, Naskh, Thuluth, Nastaliq), elaborate geometric and arabesque ornamentation respecting aniconic artistic traditions, and sophisticated miniature painting traditions particularly in Persian, Mughal, and Ottoman court manuscripts.

1.1.3 Palm Leaf Manuscripts: The Distinctive Manuscript Tradition of South and Southeast Asia

Figure **Error! No text of specified style in document.**.1: Rare manuscripts bring alive India's wide historical connect across Asia

Among these diverse global manuscript traditions, palm leaf manuscripts occupy a uniquely significant position as the predominant manuscript medium across South and Southeast Asia for approximately two millennia. The palm leaf manuscript tradition extended geographically from the Indian subcontinent (modern India, Pakistan, Bangladesh, Nepal, Sri Lanka) through mainland Southeast Asia (Myanmar, Thailand, Cambodia, Laos) to insular Southeast Asia (Indonesia, Malaysia, Philippines), encompassing diverse linguistic, religious, and cultural communities united by shared material culture and related scribal practices. The antiquity of palm leaf manuscript tradition remains somewhat uncertain due to the organic nature of the medium, which makes survival of very ancient examples improbable under typical tropical preservation conditions. However, textual references in ancient Indian literature including Sanskrit, Pali, and Tamil sources document palm leaf manuscript usage from at least the 5th century BCE. The Buddhist monk and scholar Yijing (635-713 CE), who traveled extensively in South and Southeast Asia, described palm leaf manuscripts in his travel accounts, indicating their widespread use across the region by the 7th century CE. The oldest surviving palm leaf manuscripts date from approximately the 9th-11th centuries CE, discovered in Nepal, Kashmir, and other regions with relatively cool, dry climates that slowed deterioration. However, the textual content of these manuscripts often reflects much earlier composition dates, indicating they represent copies of texts originally composed centuries or millennia earlier. Palm leaf manuscripts continued as the primary manuscript medium throughout most of South and Southeast Asia until the introduction of paper, which reached India via Islamic cultural transmission around the 13th-14th centuries CE but only gradually displaced palm leaves in many regions. In some conservative religious communities, particularly Buddhist monasteries in Sri Lanka, Myanmar, and Thailand, palm leaf manuscript production continued well into the 19th and even early 20th centuries despite paper availability, reflecting both tradition and the suitability of palm leaves for tropical climates.

1.2 Palm Leaf Manuscript Technology: Materials, Production Processes, and Material Culture

1.2.1 Botanical Sources and Regional Variation

Palm leaf manuscripts were manufactured from several palm species, with regional preferences reflecting local botanical availability and traditional practices. The two primary species employed were the Talipot palm (Corypha umbraculifera), a massive solitary palm native to southern India and Sri Lanka growing up to 25 meters tall with enormous fan-shaped leaves reaching 3-5 meters diameter, and the Palmyra palm (Borassus flabellifer), a shorter (10-30 meters) but more widely distributed species found throughout South and Southeast Asia. Additional species utilized in specific regions included the toddy palm (Caryota urens) in southern India, the lontar palm (Borassus sundaicus) in Indonesia, and the gebang palm (Corypha utan) in Java. These palm species share several characteristics that make them suitable for manuscript production: their leaves consist of relatively thick, fibrous tissue that when properly treated becomes durable and flexible; the leaf surface can be prepared to a smooth texture accepting inscription; and mature palms produce large leaves providing substantial writing surfaces. However, the species also present challenges: the organic composition renders them vulnerable to biological and chemical degradation; the fibrous structure creates anisotropic material properties with different strengths along and across fiber orientations; and natural variation in leaf thickness, fiber density, and surface texture creates heterogeneous substrates requiring skilled adaptation by scribes.

Figure **Error! No text of specified style in document.**.2: Talipot palm (Corypha umbraculifera),

1.2.2 Leaf Preparation Technology: From Harvested Leaf to Writing Surface

The transformation of fresh palm leaves into durable manuscript substrates involved sophisticated multi-stage processing reflecting centuries of empirical material science knowledge. While specific techniques varied across regions and communities, the general process followed a consistent framework documented in both traditional technical literature and modern ethnographic studies.

Stage 1: Leaf Selection and Harvesting - Manuscript production began with careful selection of appropriate leaves from mature palms. Traditional texts specify optimal harvesting timing, typically during particular seasons when leaf moisture content and fiber maturity reach ideal balances. Scribes preferentially selected mature leaves showing uniform color and texture without insect damage, fungal infections, or mechanical injuries that would compromise finished manuscript quality. Leaves were cut from palms using sharp implements, with traditional practices often involving ritual observances reflecting the sacred nature of texts to be written.

Stage 2: Initial Processing and Boiling - Freshly harvested leaves underwent initial processing to remove the thick midrib and trim leaves into manageable rectangular sections of standard dimensions, typically 5-8 cm width and 30-80 cm length depending on regional conventions and text requirements. These leaf sections were then boiled in water, sometimes with additives such as turmeric (Curcuma longa), which imparts antimicrobial and antifungal properties; salt, which affects osmotic properties and may help preserve leaf structure; or herbal decoctions with traditional preservative properties. Boiling served multiple functions: removing residual sap and water-soluble compounds that would otherwise promote biological degradation; partially breaking down cellular structures to increase flexibility; and beginning the process of color modification toward the desired brown or tan tones. Boiling duration ranged from 30 minutes to several hours depending on leaf thickness and desired properties.

Stage 3: Drying and Pressing - Following boiling, leaves were thoroughly rinsed in clean water to remove surface residues and then subjected to carefully controlled drying. This critical stage required balancing rapid drying to prevent mold growth against slow drying to avoid excessive brittleness and cracking. Leaves were typically hung in shaded, well-ventilated areas away from direct sunlight, which would cause uneven drying and color changes. Once leaves reached appropriate dryness (typically retaining 10-15% moisture content), they were pressed between heavy weights, often smooth wooden planks or stone slabs, to flatten them and produce uniform thickness. Pressing continued for several days to weeks, with periodic inspection and repositioning to ensure even pressure distribution.

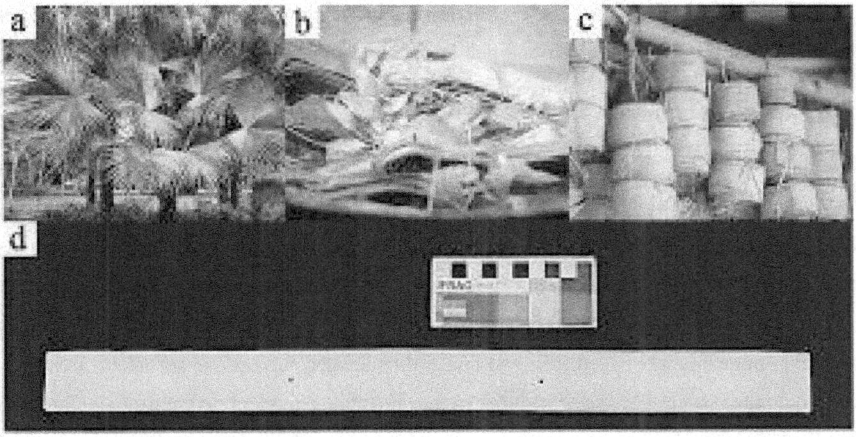

Figure **Error! No text of specified style in document.**.3 Study on the Aging Effects of Relative Humidity on the Primary Chemical Components of Palm Leaf

Stage 4: Smoke Treatment and Chemical Preservation - Dried and pressed leaves underwent smoke treatment, a distinctive and crucial preservation step largely unique to palm leaf manuscript technology. Leaves were suspended in enclosed structures and exposed to smoke from smoldering aromatic woods, resins, and herbs. Common materials included sandalwood (Santalum album), producing aromatic compounds with antimicrobial properties; sal tree (Shorea robusta) wood; and various resins. Smoke treatment served multiple preservation functions: deposition of phenolic compounds, organic acids, and other smoke constituents that inhibit fungal and bacterial growth; further moisture reduction to optimal levels; infusion of aromatic compounds deterring insect infestation; and final color development producing the characteristic warm brown tones of prepared palm leaves. Smoke treatment typically continued for several days, with leaves periodically turned to ensure uniform exposure.

Stage 5: Surface Finishing and Polishing - The final preparation stage involved surface treatment to create smooth writing surfaces. Leaves were rubbed with smooth stones, shells, or specialized tools to burnish surfaces and remove any remaining surface irregularities. Some traditions applied thin coatings of oils - coconut oil, castor oil, or specialized oil mixtures containing aromatic and preservative additives - which filled surface pores, enhanced smoothness, provided additional moisture barrier, and imparted subtle sheen. The finished prepared leaves were then stored carefully in dry conditions until needed for manuscript production.

1.2.3 Writing Technology and Inscription Techniques

Unlike manuscripts produced with ink on paper or parchment, palm leaf manuscripts employed a distinctive inscription technology reflecting the material properties of the substrate. The primary writing implement was a stylus (lekhani in Sanskrit) manufactured from metal (iron, brass, bronze, or silver depending on availability and tradition), hardened wood, or bone, shaped to a fine point suitable for incising characters. The stylus point angle, typically 20-40 degrees, represented optimization between ability to create fine detailed strokes and sufficient strength to avoid frequent breakage. The scribe held the stylus much like a modern pen, positioning it nearly perpendicular to the leaf surface, and inscribed characters through controlled pressure that engraved grooves into the leaf substrate without tearing or crushing the fibers. This incising process required considerable skill: insufficient pressure produced shallow grooves that would not adequately retain pigment and might fade quickly; excessive pressure risked tearing the leaf, particularly when inscribing across fiber orientations; and the stylus angle had to be precisely controlled to create clean, sharp edges rather than ragged, torn grooves. Experienced scribes developed remarkable fine motor control, producing characters with stroke widths as narrow as 0.3-0.5 mm. Following inscription of a complete leaf or manuscript section, the scribe applied pigment to make the incised text visible. The most common pigment consisted of fine soot (lampblack) mixed with oils or resins to create a paste. This black pigment mixture was carefully rubbed across the inscribed leaf surface, filling the incised grooves while excess remained on the unscratched surface. The leaf was then gently wiped with a soft cloth, removing pigment from smooth surface areas while leaving it embedded in the incised character grooves, creating high-contrast black text against the light brown leaf background. Alternative pigment systems included natural dyes, red ochre (sindoor), turmeric paste producing yellow text, and in some prestigious manuscripts, gold powder suspended in gum creating gold-colored characters.

The inscription technology had several consequences for palm leaf manuscript characteristics. Characters exhibit distinctive three-dimensional relief structure with depressed grooves rather than the surface deposits of ink-on-paper manuscripts, creating unique optical properties under directional lighting. Over time, especially with repeated handling or in poorly preserved manuscripts, pigment could wear away or fade, leaving only the faint incised grooves that become extremely difficult to read without proper lighting and magnification. The relief character structure also meant that both sides of each leaf could be inscribed, maximizing information density, though this also accelerated pigment wear as leaves rubbed against each other during handling and storage.

1.2.4 Manuscript Assembly, Binding, and Physical Format

Figure **Error! No text of specified style in document.**.4 Palm Leaf Engraving

Individual inscribed leaves were assembled into complete manuscripts through binding systems that balanced physical security, ease of access, and compactness. The standard South Asian palm leaf manuscript format involved piercing holes through all leaves at consistent positions, typically 3-8 cm from each end, using specialized hollow punches. Strong cords (cotton, silk, or twisted plant fibers) were threaded through these holes, stringing all leaves together in proper sequence. Wooden cover boards (phalaka), often elaborately carved or painted, were placed at the beginning and end of the leaf stack, serving both as physical protection and as decorative elements reflecting manuscript importance. The cords were secured to these boards, creating a complete bound volume. The binding allowed leaves to be flipped individually for reading while maintaining proper sequence, somewhat analogous to modern bound books but with crucial differences: unlike sewn codices where pages cannot be easily separated, palm leaf binding permitted relatively easy disassembly for individual leaf conservation or replacement of damaged leaves; the hole-and-cord system created vulnerabilities to damage, as holes gradually enlarged through repeated handling and could tear; and the binding provided minimal protection to leaf edges, which remained exposed and vulnerable to damage. Manuscript dimensions varied considerably based on text content, regional conventions, and patronage circumstances. Standard leaves typically measured 30-80 cm length × 5-8 cm width × 1-3 mm thickness. Compact manuscripts for personal use or portable religious texts might be significantly smaller (20-25 cm length), while prestigious manuscripts commissioned by wealthy patrons or institutions could reach imposing dimensions exceeding 1 meter length. The narrow leaf width dictated characteristic palm leaf manuscript typography: text was written in multiple long lines extending nearly the full leaf length (with margins of 1-2 cm at each end), typically 5-8 lines per leaf side depending on script size and leaf width.

1.2.5 Manuscript Preservation Practices: Traditional and Modern Approaches

The longevity of palm leaf manuscripts over centuries, despite their organic vulnerability, testifies to sophisticated preservation practices developed through empirical knowledge accumulation across generations. Traditional preservation methods formed integrated systems combining material treatment, environmental management, ritual practice, and periodic maintenance that together substantially extended manuscript lifespan. Traditional Oil Treatment Protocols: The most widespread preservation technique involved periodic application of natural oils to manuscript leaves, typically performed annually or biannually depending on climatic conditions and manuscript condition. The oil treatment process began with careful examination of each leaf to identify damaged sections requiring special attention. Leaves were gently cleaned using soft cloth to remove accumulated dust and particulate matter that could harbor fungal spores or insect eggs. The oil mixture-most commonly combining coconut oil as base carrier with smaller quantities of turmeric (providing antimicrobial and antifungal properties through curcumin), neem oil (strong insecticidal properties), castor oil (viscosity modification), and aromatic substances such as camphor or sandalwood oil (additional antimicrobial effects and insect deterrence)-was prepared fresh for each treatment session. Application required considerable skill: too little oil provided inadequate protection, while excessive oil could cause leaves to become sticky, attracting dust and potentially promoting mold growth in high-humidity conditions. The oil was applied sparingly using soft cloth pads or fingertips, rubbed gently across both leaf surfaces in circular motions following fiber orientations to ensure even distribution without mechanical damage. After application, manuscripts were allowed to dry in controlled conditions-typically shaded, well-ventilated spaces protected from direct sunlight which could cause uneven drying and discoloration. The drying period typically extended 24-48 hours, after which manuscripts were inspected, wiped to remove any excess oil, and returned to storage. The chemical mechanisms underlying oil treatment effectiveness involve multiple protective pathways. The hydrophobic oil coating creates a moisture barrier reducing water vapor transmission to leaf substrates, moderating the hygroscopic response to humidity fluctuations that causes dimensional instability and mechanical stress. The oils fill surface pores and microcracks, mechanically reinforcing degraded substrate while reducing sites for dust accumulation and fungal colonization. The bioactive compounds-particularly curcumin from turmeric and azadirachtin from neem-actively inhibit fungal and bacterial metabolism, creating chemical barriers to biological degradation. The aromatic volatile compounds from camphor and essential oils provide fumigant effects deterring insects through both repellent and toxic mechanisms.

Figure **Error! No text of specified style in document.**.5 Preserving memory II - documentation and digitisation of palm leaf manuscripts from Kerala, India (EAP584)

Storage Environment Management: Traditional custodians developed sophisticated understanding of optimal storage conditions, even without modern environmental control technology. Manuscripts were typically stored in specially designed wooden chests or cabinets constructed from naturally rot-resistant woods such as teak, rosewood, or sandalwood. These containers provided multiple protective functions: exclusion of light which accelerates photochemical degradation, physical barrier against dust and particulates, buffering against rapid environmental fluctuations through wood's hygroscopic properties, and aromatic wood compounds providing additional insect deterrence. Storage locations within buildings were carefully selected. Upper stories were often preferred over ground floors as they experienced lower humidity from reduced moisture wicking from soil and better air circulation. Walls facing prevailing monsoon rains were avoided to prevent moisture intrusion during heavy precipitation. Areas with good natural ventilation but away from direct window exposure balanced the need for air exchange against light exposure and dust intrusion. In temple and monastery contexts, manuscripts were often stored in dedicated rooms or alcoves considered sacred spaces, with restricted access that simultaneously served preservation by limiting handling frequency. Within storage containers, manuscripts were typically wrapped in clean cotton or silk cloth providing additional protection. Some traditions employed small sachets of camphor, cloves, black pepper, or other strongly aromatic substances placed among manuscripts to deter insects. Desiccant materials such as dried rice or specially treated clay were sometimes included to absorb excess moisture, though such practices varied regionally based on local climate patterns. Periodic Recopying and Textual Transmission: Perhaps the most effective traditional preservation strategy involved accepting manuscript impermanence and implementing systematic recopying practices. In many religious and scholarly communities, periodic recopying of important texts-typically every 50-150 years depending on usage frequency and preservation conditions-constituted standard practice. This process served multiple functions beyond mere preservation: recopying allowed correction of accumulated scribal errors through comparison of multiple manuscript witnesses, adaptation of archaic script forms to contemporary conventions improving readability for new generations, incorporation of marginal commentaries and annotations into main text where deemed valuable, and elimination of severely damaged sections through reconstruction from parallel manuscript evidence. The recopying process itself constituted significant cultural practice. In Buddhist traditions, copying sacred texts was considered highly meritorious activity (punyakarma) generating spiritual benefit for copyist, patron, and readers. The completion of major scriptural copies was often marked by celebration ceremonies, dedications, and donations to monastic communities. This spiritual dimension ensured ongoing investment in textual preservation even during periods of political upheaval or economic hardship when secular manuscript production might cease. Modern Conservation Interventions: Contemporary manuscript conservation integrates traditional knowledge with scientific analysis and advanced materials. Professional conservators employ environmental monitoring (temperature and humidity sensors, light level meters), controlled storage (climate-controlled rooms maintaining 18-22°C and 45-55% relative humidity), advanced pest management (integrated pest management using monitoring, physical barriers, and minimal chemical intervention), and physical stabilization (custom-fitted archival boxes, supportive mountings for fragile manuscripts, and minimal-intervention repair of mechanical damage). Chemical analysis techniques including X-ray fluorescence spectroscopy for ink composition analysis, Fourier-transform infrared spectroscopy for substrate degradation assessment, and chromatography for oil treatment residue characterization inform conservation decision-making. Advanced imaging modalities including multispectral imaging (capturing manuscripts under multiple illumination wavelengths to enhance faded text visibility), reflectance transformation imaging (revealing surface texture and subtle relief features), and X-ray imaging (detecting internal degradation not visible on surfaces) enable non-invasive documentation and enhance readability without physical intervention.

However, modern conservation faces substantial challenges. The specialized expertise required for manuscript conservation necessitates years of training combining art historical knowledge, materials science, and manual technical skills. The slow, labor-intensive nature of conservation work-a single damaged manuscript leaf might require several days of expert attention-creates scalability limitations when confronting collections numbering thousands or tens of thousands of items. Funding constraints particularly affect institutions in developing regions where many major manuscript collections reside, creating tragic situations where custodial institutions possess invaluable collections but lack resources for adequate preservation.

1.3 The Intellectual Content of Palm Leaf Manuscripts: Knowledge Domains and Cultural Significance

1.3.1 Religious and Philosophical Literature

Religious texts constitute numerically the largest category of palm leaf manuscripts, reflecting both the centrality of religious practice in premodern South Asian societies and the institutional support provided by temples and monasteries for manuscript production and preservation.

Hindu Religious Literature: Hindu religious manuscripts encompass extraordinary diversity reflecting the pluralistic nature of Hindu traditions. The oldest category comprises Vedic literature, including the four Vedas (Rigveda, Yajurveda, Samaveda, Atharvaveda) containing hymns, ritual formulas, and sacred knowledge dating to circa 1500-500 BCE in oral composition though committed to palm leaf form much later. Vedic manuscripts are often accompanied by auxiliary texts (Vedangas) including phonetics (shiksha), metrics (chandas), grammar (vyakarana), etymology (nirukta), astronomy (jyotisha), and ritual procedures (kalpa) that constitute technical manuals for proper Vedic recitation and ritual performance.

Figure **Error! No text of specified style in document.**.6 Veda on Palm Leaves

The philosophical Upanishads, numbering over 200 major and minor texts, present metaphysical speculations on the nature of reality, consciousness, and ultimate liberation, forming the foundation of Vedantic philosophy. Palm leaf manuscript copies of principal Upanishads often include extensive commentaries by major philosophers such as Adi Shankaracharya (8th century CE, Advaita Vedanta tradition), Ramanujacharya (11th-12th centuries CE, Vishishtadvaita tradition), and Madhvacharya (13th century CE, Dvaita tradition), with these commentarial traditions preserving distinct interpretive lineages spanning centuries.

Epic literature, particularly the Mahabharata (approximately 100,000 verses) and Ramayana (approximately 24,000 verses), exists in numerous regional recensions reflecting local narrative traditions, with palm leaf manuscripts preserving textual variants that illuminate the texts' evolution across geography and time. Puranic literature, comprising 18 major Puranas and numerous minor Puranas containing mythological narratives, cosmological schemes, genealogies, and sectarian teachings, circulated extensively in palm leaf format, with different Puranas emphasized in different regional and sectarian contexts. Devotional literature (bhakti) in regional languages-including Tamil Nayanar and Alvar hymns, Kannada Vachanas, Telugu prabandhas, and Marathi abhangas-represents vernacular religious expression often challenging Sanskrit brahmanical orthodoxy [1], with palm leaf manuscripts preserving this democratizing spiritual movement. Tantric texts describing esoteric rituals, meditative practices, and philosophical systems circulated primarily through manuscript transmission within initiated lineages, with many manuscripts featuring elaborate diagrams (yantras) and visualizations (mandalas) essential to tantric practice.

Buddhist Literature: Buddhist palm leaf manuscripts constitute among the oldest surviving examples, with manuscripts from Nepal and Tibet dating to 9th-11th centuries CE. The Buddhist canon (Tripitaka) comprises three "baskets": Vinaya Pitaka containing monastic disciplinary rules, Sutta Pitaka (Sutra Pitaka in Sanskrit) preserving discourses attributed to the Buddha, and Abhidhamma Pitaka (Abhidharma Pitaka) presenting systematic philosophical and psychological analysis. Pali manuscripts from Theravada Buddhist traditions in Sri Lanka, Myanmar, Thailand, Cambodia, and Laos preserve canonical texts in Pali language using regional scripts. These manuscripts often feature elaborate decorative elements including gilt lettering, painted illustrations, and ornamental covers reflecting the high esteem accorded to Buddha's teachings. Sanskrit Buddhist manuscripts, particularly from Mahayana and Vajrayana traditions, preserve texts including Prajnaparamita (Perfection of Wisdom) sutras, Lotus Sutra, Avatamsaka Sutra, and philosophical treatises by major Buddhist thinkers such as Nagarjuna, Asanga, Vasubandhu,

Dharmakirti, and Shantideva. Commentarial literature, comprising atthakatha (commentaries) and tika (sub-commentaries) in Pali tradition and shastra texts in Sanskrit tradition, represents scholarly engagement with canonical texts spanning centuries, with manuscripts preserving exegetical lineages and interpretive debates. Esoteric Vajrayana texts (tantras), particularly preserved in Tibetan and Nepalese collections, describe complex ritual systems, deity visualizations, and meditative practices, often accompanied by detailed painted illustrations (thangkas) when manuscripts were commissioned by wealthy patrons.

Figure **Error! No text of specified style in document.**.7 Early Buddhist Manuscript Painting: The Palm-Leaf Tradition

Jain Literature: Jain manuscripts, produced by one of the world's oldest religious communities emphasizing non-violence (ahimsa), asceticism, and liberation through knowledge, constitute major collections particularly in western and southern India. The Jain canon (Agamas) comprises texts in Prakrit languages (Ardhamagadhi, Maharashtri, Shauraseni) preserving teachings attributed to the Tirthankaras (enlightened teachers). Digambara and Shvetambara, the two major Jain sects, maintain distinct canonical collections reflecting ancient schism over monastic practices and textual authenticity. Jain manuscripts are notable for elaborate illuminated illustration traditions, with many manuscripts featuring detailed paintings in vibrant mineral pigments depicting cosmological diagrams, Tirthankara biographies, and narrative episodes from Jain sacred history. The aesthetic refinement of Jain manuscripts reflects the economic prosperity of Jain merchant communities who were major manuscript patrons, often commissioning luxurious copies as acts of religious merit.

Figure **Error! No text of specified style in document.**.8 Leaf from a Jain Manuscript: Kalpa-sutra: text (verso)

1.3.2 Scientific and Technical Literature

Beyond religious content, palm leaf manuscripts preserve sophisticated technical knowledge across multiple scientific domains, challenging outdated stereotypes of premodern societies as scientifically unsophisticated.

Medical Literature (Ayurveda): Ancient Indian medical science [2], termed Ayurveda (science of life), developed comprehensive theoretical frameworks and extensive therapeutic repertoires documented in palm leaf manuscripts. The foundational texts-Charaka Samhita (circa 1st-2nd century CE, focusing on internal medicine), Sushruta Samhita (circa 6th century BCE - 5th century CE, specializing in surgery), and Ashtanga Hridaya (circa 7th century CE, systematizing earlier knowledge)-describe physiological systems based on three humors (doshas), disease etiology and pathogenesis, diagnostic techniques including pulse examination, and therapeutic modalities encompassing diet, herbs, minerals, and surgical procedures. The Sushruta Samhita documents over 300 surgical procedures including rhinoplasty (nasal reconstruction), cataract surgery, cesarean section, and fracture management, alongside descriptions of 121 surgical instruments with their manufacturing specifications. Manuscripts preserve detailed botanical descriptions of thousands of medicinal plants including habitat, morphological characteristics, preparation methods, dosages, therapeutic indications, and contraindications. Regional medical traditions developed specialized texts addressing local disease patterns and indigenous pharmacopeias, with manuscripts in Tamil (Siddha medicine tradition) [3], Malayalam (Kerala Ayurveda), and Tibetan (incorporating Indian [4], Chinese, and indigenous medical knowledge) preserving distinctive theoretical and therapeutic approaches. Astronomical and Mathematical Literature: South Asian astronomical traditions, termed Jyotisha (science of celestial bodies), developed sophisticated mathematical astronomy producing accurate predictions of planetary positions, eclipses, and calendrical calculations. Major astronomical texts preserved in palm leaf manuscripts include the Aryabhatiya by Aryabhata (476-550 CE) presenting planetary parameters, trigonometric tables, and mathematical methods, the Brahmasphutasiddhanta by Brahmagupta (598-668 CE) advancing

Figure **Error! No text of specified style in document.**.9 Palm leaf manuscript sample

algebraic methods and astronomical models, and numerous regional karanas (astronomical handbooks) and panchanga (almanacs) providing practical computational procedures. These texts document several notable mathematical achievements: systematic use of decimal place-value notation with zero symbol (predating similar European developments by centuries), sophisticated trigonometric methods including sine tables calculated to high precision, combinatorial mathematics and early probability theory, and algebraic methods solving indeterminate equations. Manuscripts often feature extensive numerical tables, diagrams illustrating geometrical constructions and astronomical configurations, and worked examples demonstrating computational procedures.

Grammatical and Linguistic Literature: The Sanskrit grammatical tradition, culminating in Panini's Ashtadhyayi (circa 5th-4th century BCE), represents one of history's most sophisticated linguistic analyses, describing Sanskrit phonology, morphology, and syntax through approximately 4,000 concise rules (sutras) employing sophisticated metalinguistic notation. Palm leaf manuscripts preserve this foundational text alongside extensive commentarial traditions including the Mahabhashya by Patanjali (circa 2nd century BCE) and numerous later commentaries explicating Panini's dense formulations. Regional language grammars modeled on Sanskrit grammatical methodology describe Prakrit, Tamil, Kannada, Telugu, and other languages, with manuscripts documenting the evolution of linguistic analysis across different language families. Lexicographical works (kosha in Sanskrit) provide organized vocabularies with synonyms, homonyms, and semantic classifications, serving both practical reference functions and theoretical investigations of meaning and categorization.

Figure **Error! No text of specified style in document.**.10 Panini's Ashtadhyayi

Architectural and Artistic Treatises: Technical manuals (shastras) describing temple architecture, sculpture, painting, music, and dance preserve sophisticated aesthetic theories and practical construction/performance methodologies. The Shilpa Shastras detail temple proportional systems based on geometric and numerical relationships, iconographic specifications for deity images, construction techniques for different structural elements, and ritual procedures for temple consecration. The Natya Shastra, attributed to Bharata Muni (circa 200 BCE - 200 CE), constitutes comprehensive treatise on dramatic theory and stagecraft, describing performance techniques, emotional expression (rasa theory), dance forms, musical modes, and theatrical production. These technical texts illuminate the theoretical foundations underlying premodern artistic production, revealing that what might appear to modern observers as folk traditions often operated within sophisticated theoretical frameworks transmitted through manuscript-based learning.

1.4 Evolution and Characteristics of Indic Scripts in Palm Leaf Manuscripts

1.4.1 The Brahmic Script Family: Origins and Diversifications

The scripts employed in palm leaf manuscripts [5] across South and Southeast Asia belong to the Brahmic (or Indic) script family, tracing their ancestry to the ancient Brahmi script that emerged in the Indian subcontinent circa 3rd century BCE during the Mauryan Empire. The historical development and diversification of Brahmic scripts represents one of the most extensive script evolution processes in human history, with a single ancestral writing system giving rise to dozens of distinct modern scripts [6] used by billions of people across multiple language families.

Brahmi Script: The Common Ancestor: Brahmi script, first attested in substantial corpus through Emperor Ashoka's rock and pillar edicts (circa 268-232 BCE), appears as a fully developed writing system without clear intermediate developmental stages preserved in archaeological record. This sudden appearance has generated scholarly debate regarding Brahmi's origins, with competing hypotheses proposing indigenous Indian development versus derivation from Semitic scripts (Aramaic, Phoenician) used in Persian Empire administration, or synthesis combining indigenous symbols with organizational principles borrowed from west Asian writing systems.

Figure **Error! No text of specified style in document.**.11 Brahmi Script

Brahmi possessed several distinctive structural features that it transmitted to descendant scripts. It was fundamentally an abugida (alphasyllabary) where each consonant letter carried inherent vowel /a/, modified through diacritical marks to represent other vowels, contrasting with pure alphabets where consonants and vowels receive equal independent representation. The directionality was consistently left-to-right, unlike its possible Semitic precursors which employed right-to-left writing. The character inventory included approximately 46 basic symbols representing consonants (with inherent /a/), independent vowel forms used word-initially, and vowel diacritics (matras) attached to consonants for vowel modification.

Geographic and Temporal Diversification: From the 3rd century BCE through 5th century CE, Brahmi script underwent gradual evolution visible in inscriptions from different regions and periods. Character forms became increasingly cursive with simplified strokes replacing earlier angular constructions, regional variants emerged as local scribal practices diverged in different kingdoms and cultural zones, and additional characters were developed to represent sounds present in regional languages but absent in original Sanskrit phonology. By the 5th-7th centuries CE, this diversification had crystallized into distinct regional scripts that scholars classify into two major branches based on paleographic characteristics. The Northern Brahmi branch developed in northern and central India, evolving through intermediate forms (Gupta script circa 4th-6th centuries CE, Siddham script circa 6th-13th centuries CE) into medieval scripts including Nagari (precursor to Devanagari), Sharada (Kashmir and northwestern regions), and various regional scripts of northern India. The Southern Brahmi branch evolved in peninsular India and

Sri Lanka, developing through early forms such as Tamil-Brahmi and Bhattiprolu script into medieval scripts including Grantha (for Sanskrit in Tamil Nadu), Kadamba-Chalukya script (western Deccan), Pallava-Grantha script (eastern coast), and early forms of modern South Indian scripts [7].

1.4.2 Detailed Characteristics of Target Scripts

This research focuses on four major Indic scripts extensively represented in palm leaf manuscript collections: Kannada, Telugu, Devanagari, and Tamil. Understanding their paleographic characteristics, evolutionary trajectories, and distinctive features is essential for appreciating the computational challenges of script classification and character recognition.

Telugu Script: Evolution and Distinctive Features

Telugu script shares common ancestry with Kannada through Kadamba-Chalukya script lineage, leading to substantial visual similarity that creates classification challenges. The divergence began around 7th-8th centuries CE as Telugu and Kannada literary cultures developed distinct identities under different political patronage, with scripts co-evolving with their respective literary traditions. Early Telugu script, termed Telugu-Kannada script by some paleographers, remained nearly indistinguishable from contemporary Kannada script until approximately 11th century CE. Subsequent evolution produced increasingly distinct forms, though sufficient similarities persisted that even trained paleographers occasionally misidentify manuscripts, particularly those from transitional periods or border regions where both languages coexisted. Modern Telugu script exhibits rounded, cursive character forms similar to Kannada but with subtle distinctive features. Comparative analysis reveals several differentiating characteristics: certain consonants show consistent stroke difference (Telugu 'da' exhibits more pronounced circular element compared to Kannada equivalent), vowel diacritics employ slightly different positioning and proportions (Telugu /e/ and /ai/ marks extend further leftward), compound character formation follows somewhat different aesthetic principles with Telugu preferring more integrated fusion versus Kannada's more distinct component preservation, and overall character proportions tend toward slightly greater vertical extension in Telugu versus Kannada's more equidimensional proportions. The phonological inventory parallels Kannada with same 49 basic consonants, 13 vowels, and extensive compound character system. Historical Telugu manuscripts preserve additional archaic characters representing sounds lost in modern language, including specific consonant-vowel combinations and regional phonetic variants, creating paleographic complexity absent from modern printed Telugu [8].

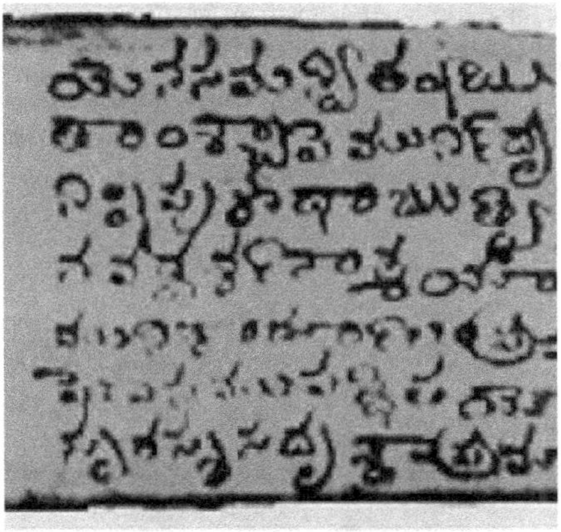

Figure **Error! No text of specified style in document.**.12 Telugu Script

Devanagari Script: Development and Characteristics

Devanagari script, employed for Sanskrit and numerous modern Indo-Aryan languages including Hindi, Marathi, and Nepali, evolved from Northern Brahmi lineage through Gupta script (4th-6th centuries CE) and Nagari script (8th-11th centuries CE). The term "Devanagari" (literally "divine city script") emerged around 12th century CE, though the script's standardization continued through medieval period. Devanagari presents distinctive paleographic characteristics clearly differentiating it from South Indian scripts. The most prominent feature is the horizontal headline (śirorekha) connecting characters within words, creating continuous upper boundary absent in South Indian scripts' disconnected character forms. Character shapes employ more angular constructions with straight vertical stems, sharp turns, and geometric regularity contrasting with South Indian scripts' curved, flowing aesthetics. The character inventory comprises 33 basic consonants (representing sounds common in Sanskrit and Hindi) plus additional characters for sounds specific to Sanskrit, Persian-Arabic loanwords, and regional languages. Vowel representation follows standard Indic pattern with independent forms for word-initial position and diacritical modifications for post-consonantal position, but Devanagari vowel marks employ different spatial positioning than South Indian scripts. Devanagari compound characters

(संयुक्ताक्षर, saṃyuktākṣara) form through several mechanisms: vertical stacking (common pattern where second consonant appears below first), horizontal juxtaposition with characters maintaining relatively distinct forms connected by headline, and special half-forms (अर्धाक्षर, ardhākṣara) where specific consonants take abbreviated shapes when appearing as first element of compound. The virama diacritic (हलन्त, halanta) explicitly marks consonant lacking inherent vowel, providing disambiguation mechanism not universally employed in all Indic scripts.

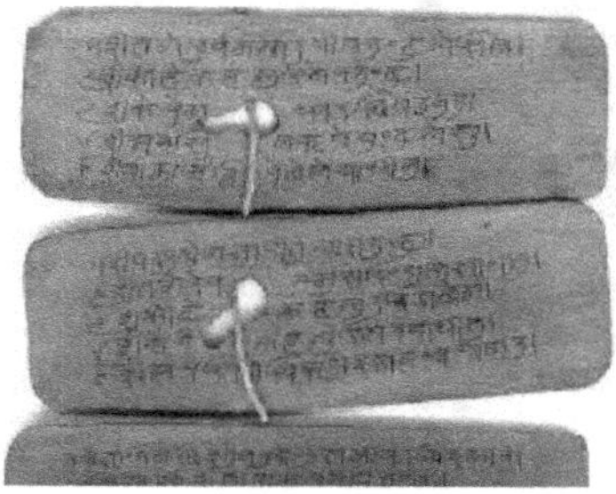

Figure **Error! No text of specified style in document.**.13 Devanagari Script

Tamil Script: Conservative Features and Distinctiveness

Tamil script, among the oldest continuously used writing systems, preserves several archaic features reflecting its conservative evolution from early Southern Brahmi (Tamil-Brahmi, circa 3rd century BCE - 5th century CE). Unlike other major Indic scripts that underwent substantial medieval transformation, Tamil script maintained relatively stable character forms from medieval period (7th-8th centuries CE) through present, though palm leaf manuscript paleography differs from modern printed Tamil. Tamil's most distinctive feature is its reduced consonant inventory comprising only 18 basic consonant letters, contrasting dramatically with 33-49 consonants in other Indic scripts. This reduction reflects Tamil phonology's deliberate avoidance of Sanskrit borrowings and preference for native phonetic patterns. The 18 consonants represent: 6 stop consonants in three points of articulation (velar, dental, alveolar: ka, ṅa, ca, ña, ṭa, ṇa, ta, na, pa, ma), 4 sonorants (ya, ra, la, va, l̲a, ḷa), and additional consonants, with aspirated consonants and several Sanskrit phonetic categories completely absent from native Tamil consonant inventory. Vowel representation employs 12 vowel forms (a, ā, i, ī, u, ū, e, ē, ai, o, ō, au) with corresponding diacritics, following standard Indic alpha syllabary pattern. The character aesthetics emphasize rounded, curved forms with substantial white space within characters, creating open, airy visual appearance distinct from other scripts' denser constructions. Tamil's treatment of Sanskrit loanwords, ubiquitous in religious and learned literature, creates orthographic complexity. Sanskrit sounds absent from native Tamil phonology are represented through special marker (ஆய்தம், āytam) or combinations of existing Tamil characters following systematic but complex conventions, requiring readers to recognize Sanskrit etymologies to correctly pronounce written words.

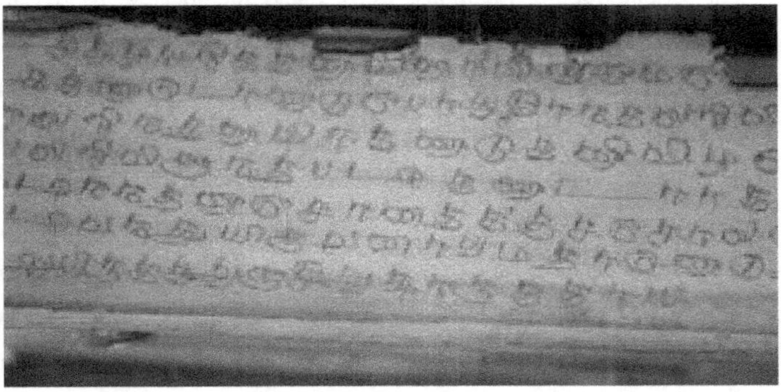

Figure **Error! No text of specified style in document.**.14 Tamil Script

Compound characters form less extensively than in other Indic scripts due to Tamil's phonological structure preferring vowel insertion between consonants, but compounds do occur particularly in Sanskrit loanwords, with formation following stacking patterns similar to other South Indian scripts.

1.4.3 Paleographic Variation in Palm Leaf Manuscripts

Beyond differences between scripts, substantial paleographic variation exists within each script across temporal, geographic, and institutional dimensions. Understanding this variation is crucial for developing robust recognition systems that generalize across diverse manuscript sources. Temporal Evolution: Scripts evolved continuously throughout the palm leaf manuscript period (approximately 9th-19th centuries CE for surviving examples) [9][10]. Character forms underwent gradual modification: letter proportions shifted with certain strokes becoming relatively longer or shorter, stroke curvature increased over time producing progressively more cursive forms, decorative embellishments were added particularly in prestigious manuscripts, and new compound character variants emerged as scribal conventions evolved. A manuscript from 12th century CE exhibits systematically different character forms than 18th century manuscript in same script, potentially confusing recognition systems trained predominantly on one temporal period. Geographic Variation: Regional scribal traditions developed distinctive paleographic characteristics even within single script. Kannada manuscripts from northern Karnataka (historical Kalyana region) show subtle but consistent differences from those produced in southern Karnataka (Mysore region), reflecting distinct political and cultural centers with independent scribal training traditions. Coastal and interior regions developed variant forms, border regions between script zones (Telugu-Kannada transition area in eastern Karnataka/western Andhra Pradesh) produced hybrid forms exhibiting characteristics of both scripts, and kingdoms with distinctive court cultures fostered unique calligraphic styles associated with royal patronage. Institutional Context: Manuscripts produced in different institutional contexts exhibit systematic stylistic differences. Temple manuscripts intended for ritual recitation emphasize clarity and regularity to ensure accurate performance, monastic manuscripts for scholarly study often include elaborate commentarial annotations in smaller scripts creating complex page layouts, personal manuscripts copied by individuals for private use show more variable quality and idiosyncratic forms [11], and commercial manuscripts produced by professional scribes for sale represent standardized, efficient writing optimizing production speed.

Scribal Idiosyncrasy: Individual scribes developed personal writing styles analogous to modern handwriting variation. Experienced professional scribes achieved remarkable consistency and elegance, novice scribes produced irregular, hesitant forms with variable stroke thickness and spacing, elderly scribes or those with visual impairment created characters with distinctive tremor patterns, and hasty copying produced abbreviated or simplified forms sacrificing aesthetic refinement for speed.

This multidimensional variation creates substantial challenges for automatic script classification and character recognition, requiring training datasets that capture representative diversity across all variation axes.

1.5 Palm Leaf Manuscript Degradation: A Comprehensive Analysis

1.5.1 Environmental Degradation Mechanisms

Palm leaf manuscripts, as organic materials composed primarily of cellulose, hemicellulose, lignin, and associated biochemical compounds, are inherently vulnerable to environmental degradation through multiple interacting physical, chemical, and biological processes.

Humidity-Driven Degradation: The hygroscopic nature of cellulosic materials means palm leaves continuously exchange moisture with surrounding atmosphere, with equilibrium moisture content determined by relative humidity and temperature. In typical tropical environments where most manuscripts have been stored (60-85% relative humidity), palm leaves maintain moisture contents of 12-18%, sufficient to support biological activity. Cyclic humidity fluctuations cause repeated dimensional changes as leaves swell when absorbing moisture and shrink during drying, inducing mechanical stress that progressively weakens fiber structure. Daily cycles (following diurnal temperature variations affecting relative humidity) accumulate thousands of stress cycles annually, while seasonal monsoon cycles impose larger magnitude changes. The anisotropic structure of palm leaves, with stronger mechanical properties along fiber orientation than across fibers, causes differential expansion and contraction leading to warping, curling, and eventual cracking perpendicular to fiber direction. High absolute humidity provides optimal conditions for fungal growth, with most cellulolytic fungi requiring >65% relative humidity and >10% substrate moisture content for active metabolism. Once established, fungal hyphae penetrate leaf tissue secreting cellulase and hemicellulase enzymes that break down structural polysaccharides into simple sugars for fungal nutrition, creating progressive substrate degradation. Visible manifestations include characteristic brown spots (foxing) from fungal metabolites, white powdery surface growth (active fungal colonies), and substrate softening and loss of mechanical integrity in severely infected regions.

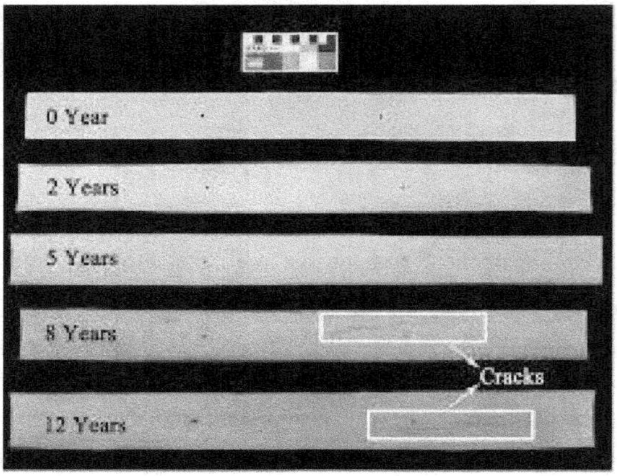

Figure **Error! No text of specified style in document.**.15 Photographs of samples after storage for 0, 2, 5, 8, and 12 years.

Temperature Effects: Elevated temperatures accelerate chemical degradation processes following Arrhenius kinetics, where reaction rates approximately double for each 10°C temperature increase. Tropical storage conditions (28-35°C typical ambient temperatures) impose substantially faster degradation rates than temperate climate storage (15-25°C), creating geographic disparities in manuscript preservation states. Temperature fluctuations, particularly when coupled with humidity changes, exacerbate mechanical stress through differential thermal expansion. Extreme temperatures have direct destructive effects: fire damage from accidents or warfare causes immediate catastrophic loss, while prolonged exposure to direct sunlight creates localized heating plus ultraviolet radiation effects (discussed below).

Light and Photochemical Degradation: Exposure to natural and artificial light, particularly ultraviolet and short-wavelength visible radiation, drives photochemical reactions that progressively degrade organic materials. UV radiation (280-400 nm wavelength) possesses sufficient energy to break chemical bonds in cellulose, hemicellulose, lignin, and ink compounds, creating free radicals that propagate chain reactions fragmenting polymer molecules. Visible light, though less energetic than UV, produces photochemical effects through prolonged exposure. Blue and violet wavelengths (400-500 nm) are particularly damaging relative to their intensity. The cumulative effect of light exposure manifests as characteristic yellowing and browning of palm leaves, progressive fading of ink until text becomes barely visible or completely illegible, substrate brittleness from cellulose polymer chain scission, and increased susceptibility to mechanical damage as chemical degradation weakens fiber structure. Traditional storage in wooden chests provided substantial light protection, but manuscripts removed for reading or display suffer accelerated photochemical degradation. Modern digitization, ironically intended for preservation, exposes manuscripts to intense illumination during scanning, potentially adding measurable degradation unless carefully controlled short-duration exposure protocols are employed.

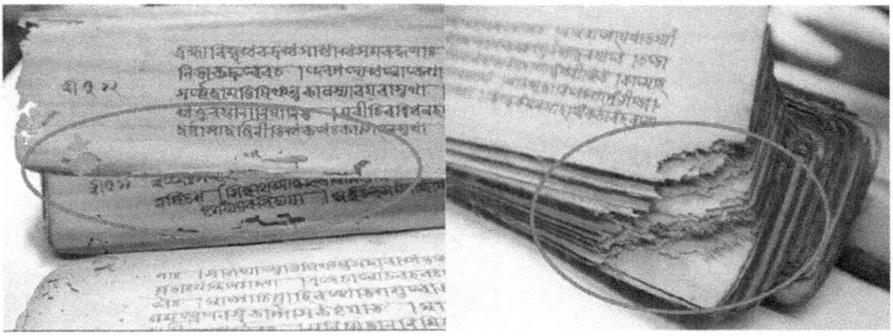

Figure **Error! No text of specified style in document.**.16 Damaged palm leaves

1.5.2 Biological Degradation

Fungal Degradation: Fungal organisms represent the primary biological threat to palm leaf manuscripts in humid tropical environments. The fungi most commonly isolated from degraded manuscripts include species from genera Aspergillus, Penicillium, Fusarium, Cladosporium, Alternaria, and Trichoderma, most of which possess cellulolytic capabilities. The fungal life cycle on manuscripts begins with spore deposition from airborne dispersal. Under favorable conditions (adequate humidity, appropriate temperature, presence of nutrients), spores germinate extending hyphal filaments that penetrate leaf surface. The growing mycelium secretes enzymes including exoglucanases that cleave glucose units from cellulose chain ends, endoglucanases that randomly hydrolyze interior cellulose bonds, and β-glucosidases that convert cellobiose and short oligosaccharides to glucose. Additional enzymes degrade hemicellulose (xylanases, mannanases) and lignin (laccases, peroxidases), achieving complete decomposition of lignocellulosic substrate. Visible fungal damage presents diverse appearances depending on species and growth conditions. Brown foxing spots result from fungal metabolites (primarily melanin and related compounds) that diffuse into surrounding substrate creating permanent discoloration persisting even after fungal death. White or colored surface growth indicates active fungal colonies that can be mechanically removed though underlying degradation remains. Localized soft spots and holes indicate advanced degradation where fungal metabolism has destroyed substrate mechanical integrity. Black staining sometimes results from particularly pigmented fungal species or fungal growth on iron-containing substrates.

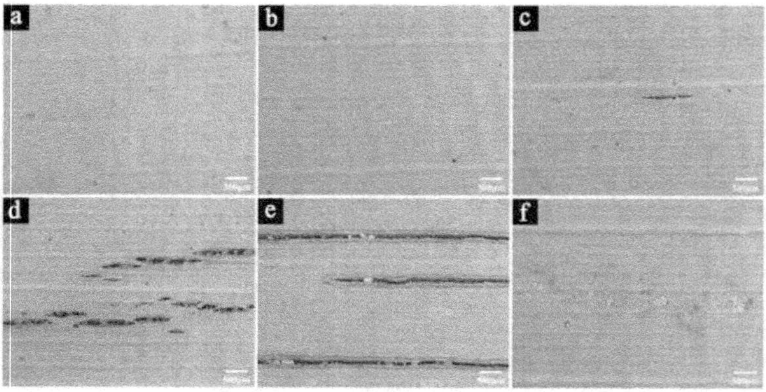

Figure **Error! No text of specified style in document.**.17 The microscopic images of the newly prepared samples (a) and samples naturally aged for 2 years (b), 5 years (c), 8 years (d), and 12 years (e,f).

Insect Damage: Multiple insect species attack stored manuscripts consuming substrate material for nutrition. Silverfish (Lepisma saccharina and related species) feed on carbohydrates including cellulose, creating characteristic irregular holes and surface grazing patterns. Booklice (Liposcelis species) consume fungal growth and mold but also damage substrate, thriving in humid conditions that support both fungi and booklice populations in destructive synergy. Various beetle larvae bore through manuscripts creating clean-edged circular holes and internal tunnels. Termites, though primarily targeting wooden storage furniture, occasionally attack manuscripts particularly if stored in ground-level locations accessible to subterranean termite colonies. Insect damage differs from fungal degradation in producing physical material loss (holes, channels, missing sections) rather than in-situ chemical transformation. The mechanical disruption is often more immediately destructive than fungal effects, with single insect infestation destroying multiple leaves within weeks. Insect excrement deposits also create staining and provide nutrient sources encouraging subsequent fungal growth.

Bacterial Degradation: Though less studied than fungal effects, bacterial degradation contributes to manuscript deterioration particularly under very high humidity conditions. Cellulolytic bacteria including Cellulomonas, Cytophaga, and various actinomycetes colonize moist substrates secreting cellulase enzymes. Bacterial degradation often produces slime layers, mucilaginous surface coatings, and unpleasant odors from volatile metabolic byproducts. The relative contribution of bacteria versus fungi to manuscript degradation remains unclear with both often coexisting in complex microbial communities.

1.5.3 Chemical Degradation Processes

Acid Hydrolysis: Cellulose and hemicellulose polymers undergo acid-catalyzed hydrolysis breaking glycosidic bonds linking sugar units. This process occurs even in neutral conditions through slow autocatalytic reactions, but accelerates dramatically in acidic environments. Sources of acidity include atmospheric pollutants (sulfur dioxide, nitrogen oxides) that dissolve in moisture forming sulfuric and nitric acids, degradation byproducts from cellulose breakdown itself creating auto-catalytic cycles, and iron-containing inks or treatments that undergo hydrolysis releasing iron ions catalyzing oxidation reactions producing organic acids. The consequence of acid hydrolysis is progressive polymer chain scission reducing average molecular weight and degree of polymerization. As cellulose chains shorten, substrate mechanical properties deteriorate: tensile strength decreases making leaves prone to tearing, flexibility reduces causing brittleness and fracture under bending stress, and surface integrity weakens allowing easier fungal penetration and insect attack.

Oxidation Reactions: Cellulose, lignin, and associated compounds undergo oxidation through multiple pathways. Atmospheric oxygen reacts slowly with organic materials even at room temperature, a process accelerated by elevated temperature, light exposure (photochemical oxidation), and presence of metal ion catalysts (particularly iron and copper). Oxidation introduces carbonyl and carboxyl groups into cellulose molecules, progressively weakening glycosidic bonds and reducing molecular weight.

The visible manifestation of oxidation is yellowing and browning as chromophoric oxidation products accumulate. Advanced oxidative degradation produces extreme brittleness where leaves fracture from minimal handling stress, characteristic of severely deteriorated manuscripts centuries old.

Ink Degradation: The carbon-based inks traditionally used in palm leaf manuscripts (soot or charcoal mixed with oils) exhibit relatively good stability compared to iron-gall inks common in European manuscripts. However, even carbon inks undergo degradation through several mechanisms: oil binder oxidation and polymerization causing ink to become brittle and detach from substrate, carbon particle loss through mechanical abrasion from handling and cleaning, and photochemical degradation of binder compounds causing ink fading. In severely degraded manuscripts, ink may fade to near-invisibility while incised grooves remain faintly detectable, creating documents that appear blank to casual observation but retain recoverable text under proper lighting conditions. Specialized imaging techniques including raking light photography (illumination at shallow angles emphasizing surface relief), reflectance transformation imaging (computational processing of multiple lighting angles), and multispectral imaging (capture under multiple wavelength illuminations) can enhance visibility of such degraded text.

1.5.4 Physical Damage from Handling and Storage

Mechanical Damage from Use: Repeated handling for reading, ritual recitation, and copying imposes cumulative mechanical stress. Common damage patterns include edge wear where fingers repeatedly grasped leaves creating rounded, smoothed edges with progressive material loss, corner breaks from excessive bending stress particularly at points where binding cords penetrate leaves, surface abrasion where fingers rubbed leaf surfaces wearing away surface layers and ink, and string hole enlargement from friction as binding cords moved during handling eventually causing radial tears. Manuscripts subject to frequent ritual use (temple ceremonial texts, popular devotional works) exhibit more severe handling damage than scholarly manuscripts consulted rarely. The ironic consequence is that the most religiously important and frequently used texts often survived in worst physical condition while obscure works neglected in storage sometimes preserve excellent condition due to minimal handling.

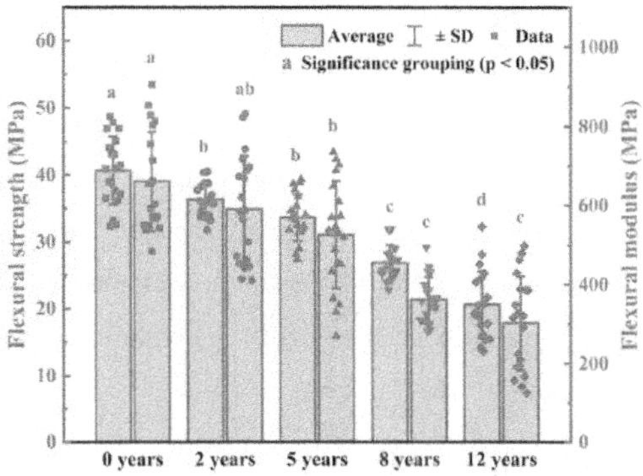

Figure **Error! No text of specified style in document.**.18 The flexural strength and flexural modulus of the naturally aged samples. Different letters indicate significant differences among groups based on Tukey's HSD test ($p < 0.05$).

Storage-Related Damage: Improper storage practices caused or exacerbated damage. Compression under heavy weight (stacking many manuscripts in piles) caused permanent deformation, particularly when combined with moisture causing plastic flow of softened substrate. Contact with hard surfaces without protective wrapping allowed mechanical abrasion. Exposure to dust and particulate matter led to surface deposits that held moisture promoting fungal growth, caused abrasive damage during page turning, and obscured text visibility. Rodent and larger animal damage occurred in poorly secured storage areas with characteristic gnaw marks, urine and fecal contamination, and nesting materials incorporating manuscript fragments.

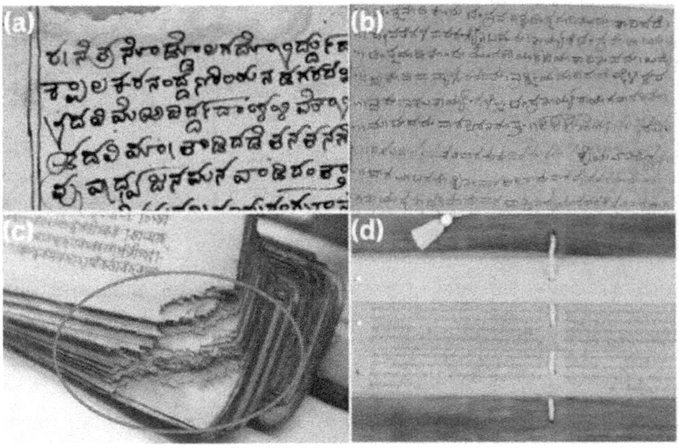

Figure **Error! No text of specified style in document.**.19 Degraged and faded manuscripts

Catastrophic Damage Events: Natural disasters and human conflicts caused sudden catastrophic manuscript loss. Flooding from monsoon inundation, river overflow, or tsunami caused immediate ink dissolution, substrate swelling and delamination, and rapid mold outbreak in wet conditions. Fire from accidental ignition, lightning strike, or deliberate destruction caused complete loss through combustion or severe thermal damage. Earthquakes caused structural collapse burying manuscripts under rubble. Warfare and civil unrest led to deliberate destruction of libraries, looting and dispersal of collections, and neglect during periods of social disruption when preservation maintenance ceased.

1.6 The Digitization Imperative: Technical Challenges and Computational Solutions

1.6.1 Rationale for Digital Preservation

Digital preservation through high-resolution imaging, computational enhancement, and automated text extraction represents the most viable comprehensive strategy for safeguarding palm leaf manuscript heritage against irreversible physical loss while simultaneously democratizing access for global scholarly communities and enabling new modes of computational analysis impossible with physical manuscripts alone.

Strategic Advantages of Digitization: Digital preservation offers multiple interconnected benefits that physical conservation alone cannot provide. Permanent archival backup creates redundant preservation copies immune to biological degradation, environmental damage, and catastrophic physical loss, with digital storage costs declining exponentially (approximately 30% annual cost reduction) while physical storage and conservation costs remain constant or increase. A single high-resolution digital image capturing manuscript appearance at specific moment provides permanent record even if original subsequently deteriorates further or is destroyed. Reduced physical handling constitutes critical preservation benefit as digitization enables unlimited virtual access without subjecting fragile originals to mechanical stress of repeated consultation. Once comprehensively digitized, original manuscripts can be stored in optimal environmental conditions (climate-controlled facilities maintaining 18-22°C temperature and 45-55% relative humidity with minimal light exposure and controlled atmospheric composition) without frequent removal for researcher access that accelerates degradation. Institutions report

80-95% reduction in physical manuscript handling requests following creation of high-quality digital surrogates, directly translating to preservation benefit. Global accessibility represents transformative democratization of scholarship, eliminating geographic and institutional access barriers that historically restricted manuscript research to scholars with physical proximity to collections. Digital libraries [12][13] enable researchers worldwide to study manuscripts without expensive travel, multi-week residence at collection sites, and dependence on institutional affiliations providing access privileges. This democratization particularly benefits scholars from developing regions who may lack funding for extensive travel, independent researchers without institutional affiliations, and graduate students unable to spend months at distant archives. Online access also enables collaborative research with multiple scholars examining same manuscript simultaneously from different locations, facilitating interdisciplinary teams combining expertise in paleography, linguistics, history, and domain content. Enhanced analysis capabilities emerge from computational processing of digital manuscript images. Full-text search across transcribed manuscripts enables rapid identification of specific passages, terms, or phrases impossible with physical

manuscripts requiring linear page-by-page examination. Linguistic analysis tools can process transcribed texts identifying grammatical patterns, vocabulary distributions, and stylistic features quantitatively. Automated indexing generates concordances, glossaries, and cross- reveals intellectual references with minimal manual labor. Paleographic analysis tools can compare character forms across manuscripts identifying regional styles [14], temporal evolution, and scribal hands.

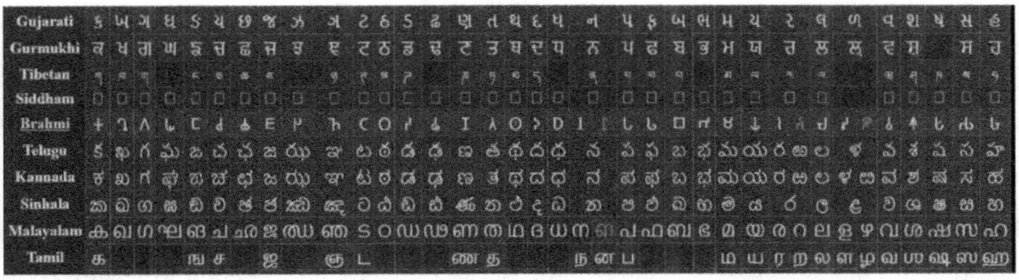

Figure **Error! No text of specified style in document.**.20 Comparison of major Brahmic scripts showing the evolution from Brahmi to modern Indic scripts (Devanagari, Telugu, Kannada, Tamil)

Network analysis of manuscript citations and textual parallels lineages and textual transmission patterns. Educational outreach becomes possible through digital access, enabling integration of primary manuscript sources into educational curricula at all levels. Students can examine actual historical documents rather than modern printed editions, experiencing materiality and paleographic challenges of manuscript-based scholarship. Virtual exhibitions and digital humanities projects make manuscript heritage accessible to general public beyond specialist scholarly communities.

1.6.2 Technical Challenges in Manuscript Digitization

Despite compelling advantages, comprehensive digitization confronts substantial technical challenges requiring specialized computational approaches beyond standard document imaging and processing workflows.

Image Acquisition Challenges: The physical capture of high-quality manuscript images involves multiple technical considerations. Resolution requirements must balance detail capture against storage costs and processing time. For accurate representation of fine textual details, character boundaries, and degradation patterns, imaging resolution should provide minimum 10-15 pixels per millimeter of actual manuscript dimension. For typical palm leaf dimensions (5-8 cm width) with character heights of 3-5 mm, this translates to image resolutions of 1500-2400 pixels vertically and 9000-24000 pixels horizontally for full leaf capture, generating individual image files of 50-200 megabytes in uncompressed format [15].

Illumination control critically affects image quality and document condition. Uniform, diffuse lighting minimizes shadows and specular reflections from leaf surfaces. However, achieving uniform illumination over large manuscript leaves requires sophisticated lighting arrays. The spectral composition of illumination affects color rendition and degradation: standard incandescent lighting generates substantial infrared radiation causing local heating and potential thermal damage, while fluorescent lighting may contain UV components accelerating photochemical degradation. LED lighting systems offer advantages of minimal heat generation, no UV emission, and tunable spectral composition, but require careful selection to ensure color rendering index >90 for accurate color capture.

Physical handling during imaging must minimize mechanical stress while achieving consistent positioning and focus. Fragile manuscripts cannot withstand pressure from glass platens used in standard flatbed scanners. Specialized manuscript scanners employ overhead camera systems with non-contact imaging, eliminating mechanical pressure but requiring careful manuscript positioning to ensure page flatness for uniform focus. Some severely deteriorated manuscripts cannot be flattened without damage, necessitating imaging with leaf curvature and subsequent computational rectification.

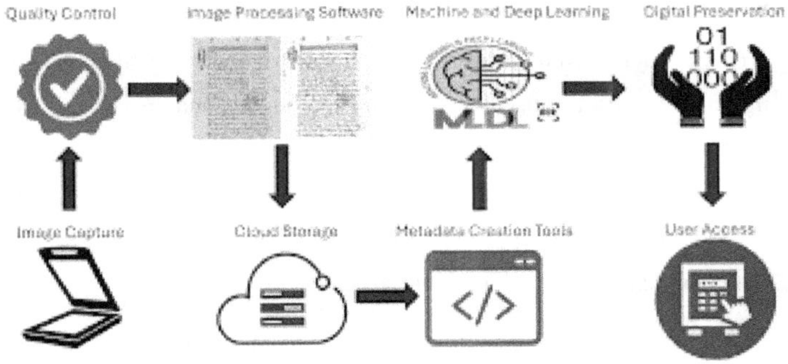

Figure **Error! No text of specified style in document.**.21 The manuscript digitization process includes various steps, initially focusing on image optimization for better clarity and readability, as well as cloud-based storage. Metadata tools and advanced technologies, e.g., optical character recognition

Color and tonal accuracy require calibrated imaging workflows using color targets, standardized illumination, and ICC color profile management to ensure consistent appearance across different viewing conditions and display devices. Uncalibrated imaging produces images where same manuscript appears different colors when captured on different occasions or equipment, complicating comparative analysis and creating misleading appearance variations.

1.6.3 Image Degradation and Enhancement Challenges

The digitized images, even when captured with optimal technical protocols, inherit and represent the degradation present in physical manuscripts, requiring computational enhancement to restore legibility.

Characteristics of Degraded Manuscript Images: Digital images of degraded manuscripts exhibit multiple problematic characteristics that impede both human readability and automated processing. Reduced character-background contrast represents the most fundamental challenge. High-quality documents exhibit character-to-background luminance ratios of 1:0.3 or higher (characters 70% darker than background), while severely degraded manuscripts may show ratios approaching 1:0.8 (characters only 20% darker than background). At contrast ratios below approximately 1:0.7, human readers experience significant difficulty, requiring intense concentration, optimal lighting, and magnification. Standard binarization algorithms designed for high-contrast printed documents fail catastrophically, producing either complete loss of faint text (threshold too high) or retention of all background noise obscuring text (threshold too low).

Spatially varying background intensity violates assumptions underlying many image processing algorithms. Substrate discoloration from age, foxing, and uneven degradation creates background that varies from near-white in well-preserved regions to dark brown in severely degraded areas within single manuscript leaf. Global thresholding cannot accommodate this variation, while local adaptive approaches may introduce artifacts if local window size mismatches actual background variation spatial scale.

Multi-modal noise patterns include multiple distinct degradation types present simultaneously. Biological staining creates irregular blob-like regions with fuzzy boundaries, fungal foxing produces circular or oval spots in various colors (brown, yellow, black) [14], physical damage causes holes and cracks with sharply defined edges, substrate texture creates fine-scale pattern from fiber structure, ink bleeding or smearing produces ghost images or doubled strokes, and scanning artifacts including sensor noise, lens aberrations, and lighting inhomogeneity add additional complexity. Effective enhancement must distinguish authentic text from diverse noise types without prior knowledge of which degradation patterns affect specific manuscript regions.

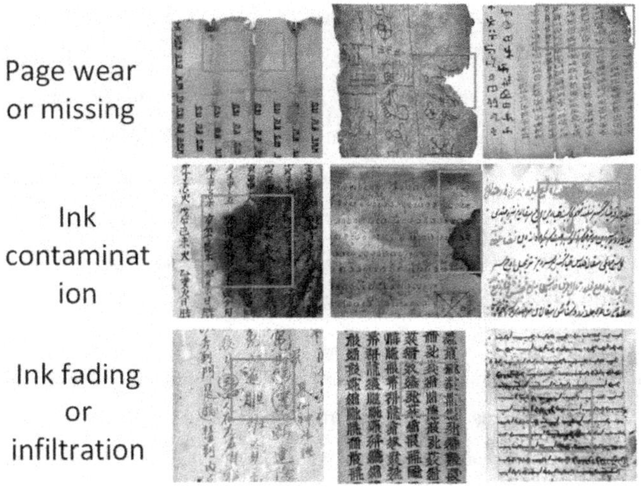

Figure **Error! No text of specified style in document.**.22 Characteristics of Degraded Manuscript Images

Character structure degradation affects textual elements themselves beyond background corruption. Ink fading produces characters with variable stroke intensity where different portions of same character exhibit drastically different darkness. Stroke fragmentation from substrate cracking causes continuous character strokes to break into disconnected segments. Edge blurring from various degradation processes destroys sharp character boundaries essential for recognition. Topological corruption, where degradation accidentally connects separate characters or breaks continuous strokes, fundamentally alters character structure in ways that simple intensity enhancement cannot address.

Limitations of Classical Image Processing: Traditional enhancement techniques developed for modern document restoration provide insufficient restoration quality for historical manuscripts.

Histogram equalization and its variants (CLAHE - Contrast Limited Adaptive Histogram Equalization) improve global or local contrast by redistributing intensity values to span full dynamic range. While simple to implement and computationally efficient, these approaches suffer fundamental limitations: they cannot restore genuinely lost information, only redistributing existing information; they amplify noise proportionally with signal, often making degradation patterns more prominent; they lack semantic understanding of text versus background, treating all image structures equivalently; and they provide no mechanism for preserving character structure beyond simple intensity transformation. Bilateral filtering and related edge-preserving smoothing techniques reduce noise while maintaining sharp boundaries by weighting spatial averaging based on intensity similarity. These methods effectively reduce uniform random noise but struggle with structured degradation patterns (stains, foxing) that resemble edges in their intensity profiles. Overly aggressive filtering blurs character boundaries defeating the purpose, while conservative filtering leaves significant degradation. Morphological operations (erosion, dilation, opening, closing) can remove small noise elements and bridge minor gaps in strokes, providing useful post-processing for binary images. However, morphological approaches require already-binarized images (creating chicken-and-egg problem of binarizing degraded images to enable morphological cleanup that might enable successful binarization), operate purely on binary geometry without intensity information, and lack adaptivity to local degradation patterns with fixed structural element sizes applied uniformly. Wavelet denoising decomposes images into multi-scale frequency representations, applies thresholding to suppress noise-dominated high-frequency components, and reconstructs filtered images. While theoretically elegant and effective for certain noise types (Gaussian white noise), wavelet methods require careful parameter tuning to distinguish noise from fine textual details that also occupy high-frequency components, perform poorly on structured non-Gaussian degradation patterns characteristic of historical manuscripts, and lack explicit modeling of character structure.

1.6.4 Deep Learning Revolution: New Paradigms for Manuscript Analysis

The emergence of deep learning, particularly convolutional neural networks (CNNs) and generative adversarial networks (GANs), has revolutionized image analysis capabilities, enabling approaches qualitatively different from classical image processing.

Convolutional Neural Networks: Learned Feature Hierarchies: CNNs learn hierarchical visual representations directly from training data through supervised learning, eliminating need for manual feature engineering. The architecture comprises multiple layers of convolution operations (applying learned filters to extract features) [16], pooling operations (reducing spatial resolution while retaining important features), and nonlinear activation functions (enabling complex non-linear mappings), culminating in fully connected layers that perform classification or regression based on learned features.

The key insight enabling CNN success is learned feature hierarchies: early layers learn low-level features (edges, corners, simple textures) automatically discovered to be useful for task at hand, intermediate layers combine low-level features into mid-level representations (character strokes, stroke junctions, character parts), and deep layers learn high-level semantic representations (complete characters, character sequences, global layout patterns). This hierarchical learning mimics hypothesized processing in primate visual cortex, achieving human-competitive performance on diverse image analysis tasks [17].

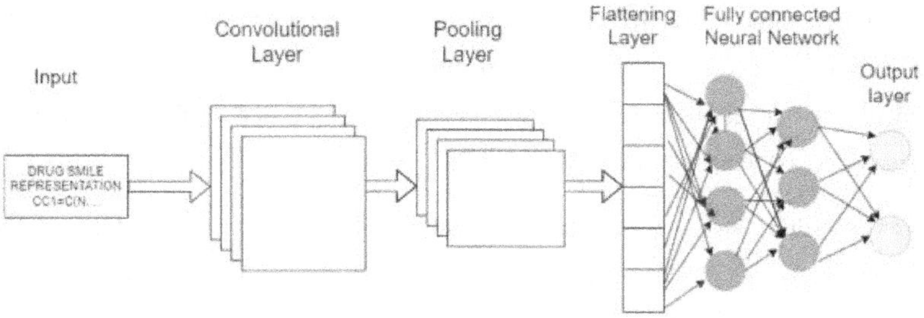

Figure **Error! No text of specified style in document.**.23 Convolutional Neural Network

For manuscript analysis, CNNs offer several advantages: they automatically learn degradation-invariant features by exposure to degraded examples during training, they capture complex non-linear relationships between input images and target outputs (classifications, enhanced images, transcriptions), and they generalize to novel degradation patterns not explicitly represented in training data through learned robust representations.

Generative Adversarial Networks: Learning to Generate and Restore: GANs represent revolutionary approach to generative modeling where two neural networks - generator and discriminator - engage in adversarial training. The generator network learns to transform input images (degraded manuscripts) into output images (enhanced manuscripts), while discriminator network learns to distinguish real enhanced manuscripts from generator outputs. Through alternating optimization, generator improves to fool increasingly sophisticated discriminator, while discriminator improves to detect generator outputs, creating training dynamic that drives both networks toward high-quality performance [18].

For image enhancement, GANs provide crucial capability: learning to generate photo-realistic enhancements that not only improve quantitative metrics (PSNR, SSIM) but also produce visually plausible results that human experts judge as natural-appearing rather than artificially processed. The adversarial training implicitly enforces constraints on output image statistics matching real enhanced manuscript distributions, preventing common enhancement artifacts like over-smoothing, halo effects around edges, and unnatural color shifts[19].

Recurrent Neural Networks and Sequence Modeling: While CNNs excel at spatial pattern recognition, recurrent neural networks (RNNs) and specifically Long Short-Term Memory (LSTM) networks address sequential pattern modeling. These architectures maintain internal state (memory) that evolves as sequential inputs are processed, enabling them to capture dependencies across temporal or spatial sequences .

For text recognition, sequences naturally arise: text lines comprise sequences of characters whose identities depend on surrounding context. Bidirectional LSTMs process sequences in both forward and backward directions, allowing each character prediction to incorporate information from both preceding and following context. This contextual integration substantially improves recognition accuracy, particularly for degraded manuscripts where local character appearance may be ambiguous but surrounding context constrains plausible interpretations [20].

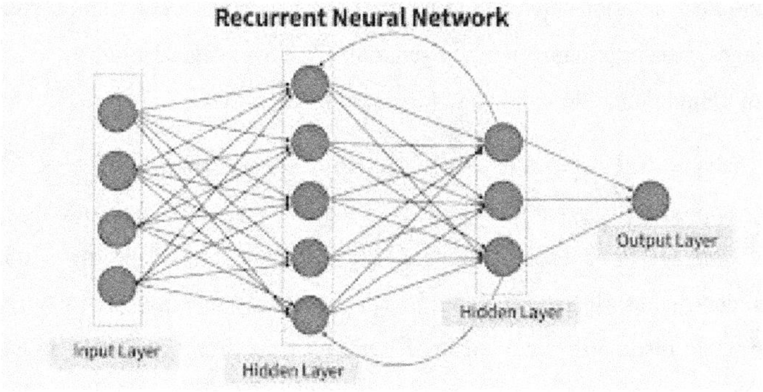

Figure **Error! No text of specified style in document.**.24 Recurrent Neural Networks

Transformer Architectures: Attention and Global Context: The transformer architecture, originally developed for natural language processing, has recently been adapted to computer vision with remarkable success. Unlike CNNs that process images through fixed receptive fields that grow gradually through layer stacking, transformers employ self-attention mechanisms that directly model relationships between all image positions simultaneously.

The attention mechanism computes, for each image position, weighted combinations of features from all other positions, with weights determined by learned similarity between positions. This enables global context modeling where distant image regions influence local processing, crucial for manuscript analysis where global layout patterns (page structure, text line orientation, inter-character spacing) provide essential context for local decisions (character classification, degradation versus text discrimination) [21].

Vision Transformers (ViT) divide images into patches (analogous to words in text), process patch sequences through transformer encoder layers learning global representations, and achieve state-of-the-art performance on image classification benchmarks. For manuscript script classification, transformers offer advantage over CNNs by directly capturing global script characteristics (overall character proportions, layout conventions, decorative elements) alongside local glyph shapes.

1.7 Research Gaps and Motivation for Present Work

1.7.1 Gap 1: Structural Preservation in Manuscript Enhancement

Existing Approaches and Limitations: Current deep learning approaches to image enhancement, while achieving impressive perceptual quality improvements, lack explicit mechanisms for preserving fine-grained structural properties essential for textual documents. Standard GAN-based enhancement optimizes adversarial loss (encouraging perceptually realistic outputs) and pixel-wise reconstruction loss (matching ground truth intensities), but neither loss directly enforces preservation of character boundaries, stroke topology, or other structural textual features. The consequence manifests in enhancement outputs that improve overall appearance and quantitative metrics but introduce subtle structural distortions problematic for subsequent analysis. Character boundaries may shift slightly or become blurred, stroke connectivity can be altered where disconnected degraded strokes are incorrectly connected or continuous strokes broken, character topology may be corrupted where loops fill in or stroke junctions separate, and fine diacritical marks crucial for character identity may disappear or shift position. For manuscript images serving subsequent computational analysis (classification, recognition, transcription), these structural distortions directly harm downstream task performance even when enhancement improves image appearance [22]. The fundamental tension arises from perceptual quality metrics emphasizing overall visual impression versus textual accuracy requiring preservation of fine structural details that may contribute minimally to perceptual quality.

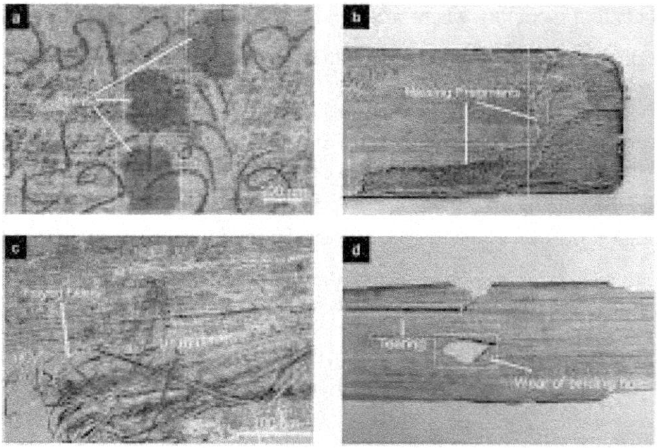

Figure **Error! No text of specified style in document.**.25 Scientific restoration of engraved palm leaf manuscripts

Prior Work Limitations: Previous research on document enhancement has employed various structural preservation approaches, but significant gaps remain. Stroke width preservation techniques enforce local stroke thickness consistency but don't address topology or boundary sharpness. Binary image refinement methods operate on thresholded images [23], requiring successful initial binarization which is the core challenge for degraded manuscripts. Character segmentation-based approaches enhance individual characters separately but require successful segmentation, again failing for degraded manuscripts where segmentation is the challenge.

No existing approach has systematically integrated edge preservation (maintaining sharp character boundaries crucial for segmentation and recognition), skeleton preservation (enforcing topological integrity preventing structural hallucinations), and perceptual quality optimization (ensuring human-acceptable visual appearance) within unified framework optimized for palm leaf manuscript enhancement specifically.

Research Contribution Needed: Development of manuscript-specific enhancement architecture incorporating explicit structural preservation constraints validated through comprehensive evaluation including crucially, downstream task performance measurement demonstrating that enhanced images improve subsequent classification and recognition accuracy compared to both unenhanced degraded images and structurally-unaware enhancement methods [24].

1.7.2 Gap 2: Vision Transformers for Degraded Indic Script Classification

Existing Approaches and Limitations: Script classification for Indic manuscripts has predominantly employed CNN-based architectures (VGGNet, ResNet, EfficientNet variants) that have achieved respectable performance on clean or moderately degraded manuscripts [24]. However, these architectures possess inherent limitations stemming from their reliance on local receptive fields that expand gradually through layer stacking but never achieve truly global field-of-view. For script classification, particularly distinguishing visually similar script pairs like Telugu-Kannada that share common ancestry and exhibit overlapping character repertoires, global contextual information provides crucial discriminative signal. Script identity manifests not merely in individual character shapes (which show substantial overlap) but in holistic characteristics: overall character density and spacing patterns, page-level layout conventions, decorative element styles, statistical distributions of character forms across page, and subtle differences in stroke aesthetics (curvature, thickness ratios, proportions) that aggregate over multiple characters. CNNs, with fixed finite receptive fields, struggle to integrate global context effectively [25]. Even deep CNN architectures with large theoretical receptive fields suffer from effective receptive field size (region actually influencing output) being substantially smaller than theoretical size, concentrating on local image regions rather than truly global integration. This local bias, while beneficial for many computer vision tasks, disadvantages CNNs for script classification where global holistic judgment by human experts often precedes detailed character-level analysis [26]. Vision Transformer Potential: Vision Transformers, through self-attention mechanisms directly modeling relationships between all image patches regardless of spatial distance, provide architectural capability for global context integration absent from CNNs. However, application to degraded historical Indic manuscripts remains largely unexplored, with existing ViT research focusing primarily on natural image domains (ImageNet classification) or clean modern documents.

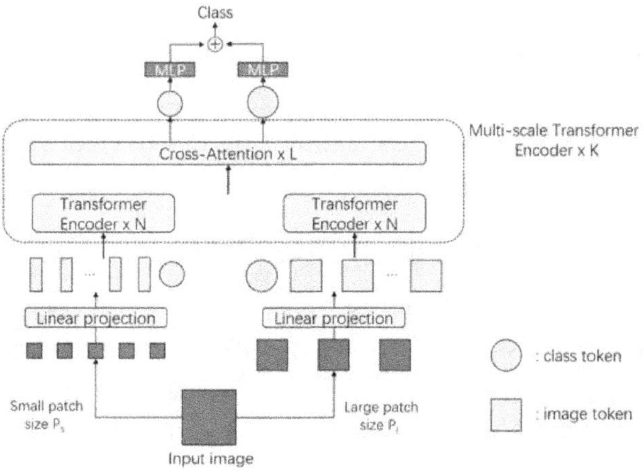

Figure **Error! No text of specified style in document.**.26 Vision Transformers for Image Classification

Several open research questions require investigation: Degradation robustness - How do transformers perform on severely degraded manuscripts where local features become unreliable and global context may provide more stable signal? Transfer learning effectiveness - Can transformers pretrained on natural images (ImageNet) effectively transfer to specialized historical manuscript domain despite dramatic domain gap? Script pair discrimination - Do transformers better distinguish confusable scripts like Telugu-Kannada through global context compared to CNNs? Architectural adaptations - What manuscript-specific architectural modifications or training protocols improve transformer performance for this specialized application. [27]

Research Contribution Needed: Systematic application of hierarchical Vision Transformers (specifically Swin Transformer architecture balancing global attention with computational efficiency) to degraded Indic script classification, with comprehensive evaluation stratified by degradation severity, per-script performance analysis revealing strengths and weaknesses, confusion matrix examination identifying specific script pair challenges, and comparative analysis against CNN baselines quantifying transformer advantages for global context-dependent discrimination [28][29].

1.7.3 Gap 3: Character Recognition Under Extreme Data Scarcity

The Data Scarcity Challenge: Modern deep learning successes overwhelmingly rely on large-scale training datasets - ImageNet (14 million images), COCO (330k images), modern OCR datasets (millions of annotated characters) [30]. However, historical manuscript analysis confronts fundamentally different data regime: extreme scarcity with training sets numbering hundreds or low thousands rather than millions [31]. For palm leaf Kannada manuscripts, comprehensive dataset creation confronts multiple bottlenecks: Expert annotation requirement - Accurate character labeling requires paleographic expertise recognizing archaic character forms, distinguishing confusable characters, and interpreting degraded ambiguous instances, with such experts numbering dozens rather than thousands globally. Annotation time cost - Manual character-level annotation averages 280 human-hours per 1,000 characters accounting for image examination, label assignment, quality verification, and ambiguous case adjudication. Inter-annotator ambiguity - Even experts disagree on severely degraded characters, with inter-annotator agreement averaging 70-75%, introducing label noise into training data. Cost and access barriers - Manuscript access requires institutional permissions, physical travel or high-resolution imaging, and funding for expert annotator time, creating project costs of thousands of dollars per thousand annotated characters. The consequence is dataset sizes of 3,000-5,000 characters for most historical script recognition projects - 1000× smaller than modern OCR training sets. With Kannada's 85-class vocabulary (49 consonants, 13 vowels, 20 common compounds, 3 modifiers), this translates to average 35-60 samples per character class - insufficient for standard deep learning requiring hundreds or thousands of samples per class for robust learning [32].

Existing Approaches and Limitations: Historical document OCR has employed various strategies for limited data scenarios. Transfer learning from modern handwriting or printed text models provides initialization but faces domain gap as historical manuscripts differ systematically from modern training domains in character forms, degradation patterns, and writing media. Data augmentation artificially expands training sets through geometric transformations, noise injection, and synthetic degradation, but conventional augmentation designed for modern documents may not capture manuscript-specific variation patterns. Few-shot learning methods attempt learning from very limited samples through meta-learning or metric learning, but existing approaches have shown limited success on complex character recognition tasks with large class sets [32].

Segmentation-Free Recognition Paradigm: Classical OCR pipelines perform explicit character segmentation followed by isolated character classification. This approach fails catastrophically for cursive scripts, touching characters, broken strokes, and degraded manuscripts where segmentation boundaries are inherently ambiguous. The segmentation-free CRNN-CTC paradigm processes entire text lines without explicit segmentation, learning implicit alignment between image sequences and character sequences through CTC loss.

While CRNN-CTC has achieved breakthrough success for modern scene text and handwriting recognition, application to historical Indic manuscripts remains limited. Key open questions include: Data efficiency - Can CRNN-CTC learn effectively from 30-50 samples per character class? Compound character handling - How do CRNN-CTC systems handle complex Indic compound characters requiring recognition of constituent components and their spatial relationships? Augmentation strategies - What augmentation approaches best capture palm leaf manuscript variation (substrate texture, ink degradation, stylus inscription characteristics) while avoiding unrealistic artifacts that harm learning? Deployment feasibility - Can models trained on scarce data achieve sufficient accuracy for practical deployment in institutional digitization workflows [33]

Research Contribution Needed: Comprehensive CRNN-CTC framework specifically adapted for historical Kannada palm leaf manuscripts under extreme data scarcity (~40 samples per class), incorporating manuscript-specific augmentation pipeline expanding effective training data 50-fold while maintaining realism, systematic evaluation stratified by character type (vowels, consonants, compounds) and degradation severity quantifying performance across difficulty axes, detailed error analysis and confusion pattern characterization identifying specific failure modes, and practical deployment validation demonstrating feasibility for institutional-scale digitization with human-in-the-loop verification of uncertain predictions.

1.8 Research Objectives:

This dissertation addresses the identified research gaps through three integrated objectives forming a complete digitization pipeline from degraded manuscript images to transcribed searchable text. Each objective tackles distinct technical challenge while contributing to overall system synergy.

1. To develop DE-GAN for structural preservation in degraded palm leaf manuscript enhancement. [Ch.3]

2. To design SwinLipi Vision Transformer for multi-script classification of Indic manuscripts. [Ch.4]

3. To implement KannadaLipi CRNN-CTC for accurate character recognition under data scarcity. [Ch.5]

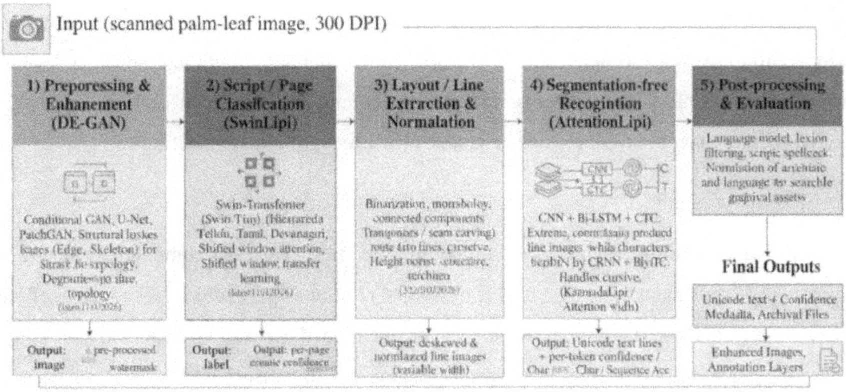

Figure **Error! No text of specified style in document.**.27 Overall architecture of the proposed palm-leaf manuscript

1.9 System Limitations and Future Directions

Current limitations requiring acknowledgment:

Language-specific focus: Current system specialized for Kannada with prototype extensions to Telugu, Devanagari, Tamil. Expanding to other Indic scripts (Malayalam, Bengali, Gujarati,

Odia, etc.) requires script-specific training data and model adaptation. Non-Indic scripts (Arabic, Persian, Tibetan manuscripts) require substantial architectural modifications.

Modern language bias: Recognition models learn character-level patterns but lack linguistic understanding of archaic grammar, vocabulary, and orthographic conventions differing from modern Kannada. This manifests as rare archaic terms misrecognized as more common modern spellings.

Compound character limitations: Compounds remain weakest performance area (71.1% accuracy). The model treats compounds as atomic symbols rather than compositional structures, requiring explicit training on each compound rather than learning component-based recognition.

Damage resilience boundaries: Extreme degradation where >50% of character area is damaged or occluded exceeds system capabilities. Characters with completely faded ink leaving only faint stylus grooves visible require specialized imaging (raking light, RTI) beyond standard photography.

Layout complexity limitations: Current system handles standard single-column text layouts. Complex layouts (multi-column texts, marginal annotations, interlinear glosses, embedded diagrams) require manual preprocessing or layout-aware recognition architectures.

Future research directions:

Compositional compound recognition: Developing models that learn compound structure as combinations of consonant components plus positional relationships, enabling recognition of rare or unseen compounds through compositional generalization. Proposed approach: Graph neural networks representing compounds as graphs of character components with spatial relationship edges.

Semi-supervised and active learning: Leveraging large quantities of unannotated manuscript images through semi-supervised learning (training on unannotated data with pseudo-labels) and active learning (iteratively selecting most informative examples for annotation) to improve performance without proportional annotation cost.

Multi-modal enhancement: Integrating multiple imaging modalities (visible light, UV, infrared, multispectral, RTI) for severely damaged manuscripts where standard imaging provides insufficient information. Deep learning fusion of multiple modalities could recover text invisible in any single modality.

Language modeling integration: Incorporating neural language models (transformer-based models trained on Kannada text corpora) for post-processing recognition outputs, correcting errors through linguistic context. Proposed: BERT-style models fine-tuned for historical Kannada suggesting corrections for unlikely character sequences.

Cross-script transfer learning: Investigating transfer learning across related scripts to bootstrap recognition for scripts with very limited training data. Hypothesis: Models trained on Kannada transfer effectively to closely related Tulu or Coorgi scripts, requiring minimal additional training.

1.10 Thesis Organization and Structure

This dissertation is organized into seven chapters presenting comprehensive treatment of palm leaf manuscript recognition through integrated computational approaches:

Chapter 1: Introduction (current chapter) establishes research context, motivation, and technical foundations. Topics covered include: manuscript heritage significance and digitization imperative, Indic script characteristics and evolution, degradation mechanisms and enhancement challenges, deep learning fundamentals for manuscript analysis, research gaps motivating present work, detailed research objectives with technical specifications, and integrated pipeline architecture.

Chapter 2: Literature Survey provides systematic review of prior work across relevant domains. Covered topics: palm leaf manuscript studies and collections, digital libraries and cataloging initiatives, existing annotated datasets for Indic scripts, image enhancement techniques for document restoration, deep learning approaches to script classification, character recognition methods from classical to modern, evaluation frameworks and benchmarking practices, identification of research gaps addressed by present work.

Chapter 3: Degraded Image Enhancement Using DE-GAN presents first major research objective. Chapter contents: detailed dataset acquisition and synthetic degradation generation, complete DE-GAN architecture specification with generator and discriminator designs, novel structural preservation losses (edge and skeleton) with theoretical justification, training protocol and hyperparameter optimization, comprehensive experimental results including quantitative metrics, ablation studies, qualitative assessment, and downstream task validation, comparative analysis against baseline enhancement methods, discussion of findings and limitations.

Chapter 4: Script Classification Using SwinLipi Vision Transformer addresses second objective. Chapter structure: introduction to script classification challenges emphasizing confusable script pairs, dataset composition including temporal, geographic, and degradation diversity, Vision Transformer and Swin Transformer architectural foundations, SwinLipi adaptation for manuscript domain including transfer learning strategy, training protocol with multi-stage fine-tuning and augmentation pipeline, experimental results with overall performance, per-script analysis, confusion matrix examination, degradation robustness evaluation, comparative analysis against CNN and traditional baselines, ablation studies validating architectural choices, discussion and analysis.

Chapter 5: Character Recognition Using KannadaLipi CRNN-CTC presents third objective. Chapter organization: character recognition challenges for historical Indic manuscripts under data scarcity, dataset composition with extreme scarcity and class imbalance, CRNN-CTC architecture with CNN feature extraction, bidirectional LSTM sequence modeling, and CTC decoding, manuscript-specific augmentation pipeline with geometric, photometric, and degradation transformations, training protocol adapted for few-shot learning, comprehensive evaluation results including overall performance, character-category stratification, degradation robustness, confusion pattern analysis, comparative baseline analysis, ablation studies, data efficiency analysis, real-world case study, discussion of contributions and limitations.

Chapter 6: AttentionLipi - Alternative Architecture Exploration presents experimental hybrid CNN-BiLSTM framework incorporating attention mechanisms for enhanced sequence modeling. This chapter explores architectural variations investigating attention mechanism benefits, comparing performance against standard CRNN-CTC, analyzing attention alignment patterns revealing model's focus, and providing insights for future architecture development.

Chapter 7: Conclusions and Future Work summarize the key contributions of this dissertation and evaluates the proposed palm leaf manuscript digitization pipeline as a unified system. It highlights the effectiveness of DE-GAN–based image enhancement, SwinLipi script classification, and KannadaLipi CRNN-CTC character recognition under severe degradation and data scarcity. The chapter discusses overall system performance and limitations, and outlines future research directions including multi-script extension, layout-aware full-page processing, end-to-end transformer-based architectures, and deployment optimization for large-scale heritage preservation.

References and Appendices furnish complete bibliographic information enabling full reproducibility, with appendices containing extended quantitative results and statistical tables (Appendix A), additional visual enhancement comparisons (Appendix B), detailed annotation guidelines and dataset documentation (Appendix C), complete implementation details and source code repositories (Appendix D), hardware specifications and training logs (Appendix E), and sample manuscript images with ground truth transcriptions (Appendix F).

This objective-centric organization ensures each research contribution receives focused treatment while maintaining clear progression from problem identification through technical solution development to comprehensive evaluation and broader impact articulation, providing both technical depth for AI researchers and practical guidance for heritage preservation practitioners.

1.11 Summary

A comprehensive introduction to palm leaf manuscripts as vital repositories of South Asian cultural heritage, detailing their historical significance, production techniques, degradation mechanisms, and digitization challenges. The chapter established the critical need for automated processing pipelines due to environmental degradation, biological deterioration, faded ink oxidation, and inconsistent scanning quality that severely compromise legibility for digital archiving and scholarly access. Research gaps in structural preservation during enhancement, Vision Transformer applications for Indic script classification, and character recognition under extreme data scarcity were systematically identified, motivating the three core objectives: DE-GAN enhancement, SwinLipi script classification, and KannadaLipi CRNN-CTC recognition forming an integrated pipeline for institutional-scale manuscript digitization.

CHAPTER 2

Literature Survey

The scholarly investigation and preservation of palm leaf manuscripts have gathered momentum over recent decades, fueled by the urgent need to preserve these invaluable cultural artifacts before time, environment, or neglect renders them inaccessible. This chapter presents a comprehensive review of existing research spanning traditional manuscript studies, digital preservation initiatives, image enhancement methodologies, script classification approaches, and character recognition systems. The literature review is organized thematically to address the three core research objectives: degraded image enhancement, script classification, and character recognition for palm leaf manuscripts.

Bendall (2001) Sanskrit Manuscripts from Nepal [1]

In this seminal work, the researcher catalogued and analyzed ancient Sanskrit manuscripts preserved in Nepal, providing detailed paleographic analysis of Brahmi script evolution from 9th-11th centuries CE. The study documented distinctive features of Nepalese manuscript tradition including substrate preparation, binding methods, and scribal conventions that influenced subsequent digitization efforts.

Losty and Roy (2012) Mughal India: Art, Culture, and Empire [2]

The authors examined manuscript production in Mughal courts, documenting illumination techniques, pigment chemistry, and patronage patterns that contextualize manuscript materiality. Their analysis of ink degradation patterns informed modern conservation strategies.

Mahadevan (2003) Early Tamil Epigraphy: From the Earliest Times to the Sixth Century CE [3]

This comprehensive study traced the evolution of Tamil-Brahmi scripts through epigraphic evidence, establishing chronological frameworks for script dating and regional variation analysis essential for paleographic classification systems.

Salomon (1998) Indian Epigraphy: A Guide to the Study of Inscriptions [4]

The researcher provided systematic methodology for analyzing Indian scripts, documenting distinctive features of Brahmic family evolution and regional adaptations that inform computational script classification approaches.

Palanivel and Rajesh Kumar (2011) The Microstructure and Composition of Palm-Leaf Manuscripts [5]

In this study, researchers employed scanning electron microscopy and X-ray diffraction to analyze palm leaf substrate composition, identifying cellulose degradation pathways and fungal colonization patterns that guided digital enhancement algorithm development.

Rajan et al. (2015) Conservation of Palm Leaf Manuscripts: Traditional and Modern Approaches [6]

The authors documented traditional oil treatment protocols and modern conservation interventions, quantifying effectiveness of various preservation strategies and establishing best practices for manuscript handling during digitization.

Aguilella-Cueco et al. (2020) Degradation Assessment of Historical Palm Leaf Manuscripts [7]

This study applied advanced spectroscopic techniques to characterize chemical degradation in aged manuscripts, revealing correlations between environmental exposure and substrate deterioration that informed synthetic degradation modeling for training data augmentation.

Sugimoto et al. (2010) Digital Library of Sanskrit Buddhist Manuscripts [8]

The researchers developed comprehensive metadata schemas for Buddhist manuscript collections, addressing multilingual cataloging challenges and establishing interoperability standards adopted by subsequent digitization projects. **National Mission for Manuscripts (2014) Cataloguing Standards for Indian Manuscripts [9]**

This initiative established standardized protocols for manuscript description, including script identification, dating conventions, and degradation assessment that enabled systematic collection management across institutional repositories.

Agosti et al. (2015) Digital Libraries for Cultural Heritage [10]

The authors surveyed digital library architectures for heritage preservation, analyzing metadata standards, access protocols, and sustainability models applicable to manuscript collections.

Gatos et al. (2006) Adaptive Degraded Document Image Binarization [11]

In this work, researchers proposed adaptive binarization algorithm combining Wiener filtering with local thresholding, achieving improved text-background separation on DIBCO benchmarks. However, the method struggled with spatially varying degradation characteristic of palm leaf manuscripts.

Su et al. (2013) Robust Document Image Binarization with OFF-center Surround [12]

The authors developed binarization technique using off-center surround background estimation and stroke-preserving filtering, demonstrating effectiveness on historical documents but requiring careful parameter tuning for manuscript-specific degradation.

Ntirogiannis et al. (2014) Combined Implementation of Document Image Binarization Techniques [13]

This study evaluated multiple classical binarization methods (Otsu, Sauvola, Niblack, Wolf) on DIBCO datasets, revealing limitations when applied to severely degraded palm leaf manuscripts with non-uniform backgrounds.

Souibgui and Kessentini (2020) DE-GAN: A Conditional Generative Adversarial Network for Document Enhancement [14]

The researchers introduced conditional GAN architecture for document image restoration, employing U-Net generator with adversarial and L1 losses. Evaluation on DIBCO datasets showed PSNR improvements but lacked explicit structural preservation mechanisms critical for manuscript character recognition.

Zhao et al. (2019) Document Image Binarization with Cascaded Generators [15]

In this study, authors proposed cascade GAN architecture progressively refining binarization through multiple generator stages, achieving state-of-art results on H-DIBCO benchmarks. The approach demonstrated improved performance on historical documents but remained untested on palm leaf manuscripts.

Tensmeyer and Martinez (2017) Document Image Binarization with Fully Convolutional Neural Networks [16]

The researchers developed fully convolutional architecture for end-to-end binarization without hand-crafted features, demonstrating effectiveness across diverse degradation types but requiring extensive training data.

Calvo-Zaragoza and Gallego (2019) A Selectional Auto-Encoder Approach for Document Image Binarization [17]

This work presented selective auto-encoder architecture learning to reconstruct clean document structure from degraded inputs, showing promising results on printed documents but limited evaluation on handwritten manuscripts.

Xiong et al. (2021) Degraded Historical Document Image Binarization Using a Conditional GAN [18]

The authors proposed conditional GAN with attention mechanisms for historical document enhancement, incorporating multi-scale processing and perceptual losses achieving competitive DIBCO performance.

Pratikakis et al. (2017) ICDAR 2017 Competition on Document Image Binarization [19]

This competition benchmark established standardized evaluation protocols for document binarization, revealing that most methods optimized for printed text performed poorly on handwritten historical documents requiring specialized approaches.

Westphal et al. (2018) Visual Enhancement of Old Documents with Hyperspectral Imaging [20]

The researchers demonstrated hyperspectral imaging for recovering faded text in medieval manuscripts, employing wavelength-specific illumination to enhance ink-substrate contrast invisible under standard imaging.

Kligler et al. (2018) Document Enhancement using Visibility Detection [21]

This study developed visibility-guided enhancement detecting locally degraded regions and applying adaptive restoration, showing improved performance on non-uniformly degraded documents.

Ghosh et al. (2010) Script Recognition: A Review [22]

The authors provided comprehensive survey of script identification techniques, documenting feature extraction methods including stroke density, directional features, and connected component analysis achieving 85-92% accuracy on multi-script printed document datasets but showing limited applicability to degraded handwritten manuscripts.

Hochberg et al. (1997) Automatic Script Identification from Document Images [23]

This pioneering work introduced texture-based features combined with k-nearest neighbor classification for script discrimination, establishing baseline methodologies that informed subsequent deep learning approaches despite performance degradation on historical documents.

Tan (1998) Rotation Invariant Texture Features and Their Use in Automatic Script Identification [24]

The researcher developed rotation-invariant texture descriptors using multichannel Gabor filtering for script classification, achieving robustness to document orientation but requiring carefully tuned filter banks limiting generalization to unseen manuscript styles.

Spitz (1997) Determination of the Script and Language Content of Document Images [25]

In this study, the author proposed script identification system based on optical density measurements and connected component statistics, demonstrating effectiveness on printed multilingual documents but failing on cursive handwritten scripts with variable character spacing.

Joshi et al. (2018) Deep Learning Based Script Identification for Indian Languages [26]

The researchers developed CNN architecture with multiple convolutional layers for classifying 12 Indian scripts, achieving 96.2% accuracy on printed text datasets. However, evaluation was limited to modern clean documents without degradation typical of historical manuscripts.

Nguyen et al. (2019) Script Identification in Natural Scene Images Using Convolutional Neural Networks [27]

This work applied ResNet-50 architecture for scene text script identification across 10 writing systems, demonstrating transfer learning effectiveness but not addressing manuscript-specific challenges including substrate degradation and ink fading.

Mei et al. (2016) Scene Text Script Identification with Convolutional Recurrent Neural Networks [28]

The authors combined CNN feature extraction with LSTM temporal modeling for script classification in natural images, showing improved performance on curved text but limited evaluation on historical document corpora.

Burie et al. (2015) ICFHR 2014 Competition on Handwritten Text Recognition on Transkribus [29]

This competition benchmark established standardized protocols for historical document analysis, revealing significant performance gaps between modern OCR systems and requirements for manuscript recognition necessitating specialized approaches.

Dosovitskiy et al. (2021) An Image is Worth 16×16 Words: Transformers for Image Recognition at Scale [30]

The researchers introduced Vision Transformer (ViT) architecture applying transformer mechanisms from NLP to computer vision, achieving state-of-art ImageNet classification with 88.5% top-1 accuracy through self-attention over image patches, establishing foundation for document analysis applications.

Liu et al. (2021) Swin Transformer: Hierarchical Vision Transformer Using Shifted Windows [31]

In this landmark work, authors developed hierarchical vision transformer with shifted window attention mechanisms enabling efficient computation and multi-scale feature aggregation, achieving 87.3% ImageNet accuracy with 4× fewer parameters than comparable CNNs, directly applicable to manuscript script classification.

Li et al. (2022) DocFormer: End-to-End Transformer for Document Understanding [32]

The researchers proposed transformer architecture specifically designed for document understanding, combining visual and textual features through self-attention achieving state-of-art results on form understanding and receipt parsing.

Xu et al. (2021) LayoutLMv2: Multi-Modal Pre-training for Visually-Rich Document Understanding [32]

This study introduced multi-modal transformer pre-trained on large document corpus, learning joint text-layout-image representations that generalized effectively to document classification and information extraction tasks.

Kim et al. (2022) OCR-Free Document Understanding Transformer [33]

The authors developed end-to-end transformer model bypassing explicit OCR, directly processing document images for classification and parsing tasks, demonstrating that transformers can learn document understanding without character-level supervision.

Huang et al. (2023) Swin-Unet: Unet-Like Pure Transformer for Medical Image Segmentation [34]

This work adapted Swin Transformer to U-Net architecture for image segmentation, showing that hierarchical transformers excel at dense prediction tasks requiring both global context and fine-grained localization relevant to manuscript character boundary detection.

Pal and Chaudhuri (2004) Indian Script Character Recognition: A Survey [35]

The authors surveyed classical pattern recognition techniques for Indic scripts, documenting handcrafted features including stroke direction, curvature, and junction points combined with template matching or structural classifiers achieving 75-85% accuracy on printed text.

Bhattacharya and Chaudhuri (2009) Handwritten Numeral Databases of Indian Scripts and Multistage Recognition of Mixed Numerals [36]

This comprehensive study established benchmark datasets for handwritten Indic numerals, evaluating SVM and MLP classifiers achieving 95%+ accuracy on isolated numerals but revealing substantial performance degradation on connected or degraded characters.

Kompalli et al. (2005) Character Recognition in Telugu Script Using Hidden Markov Models [37]

The researchers applied HMM framework to Telugu character recognition, modeling character strokes as temporal sequences achieving 82.4% accuracy on handwritten datasets but requiring explicit stroke segmentation impractical for degraded manuscripts.

Bunke and Caelli (2001) Hidden Markov Models: Applications in Computer Vision [38]

This foundational text documented HMM applications to pattern recognition including handwriting, establishing theoretical framework for sequential modeling that informed subsequent neural sequence models.

Natarajan et al. (2001) Multimodal Hidden Markov Models for Online Handwriting Recognition [39]

The authors developed multi-stream HMM integrating coordinate trajectories and pen pressure for online handwriting recognition, achieving competitive results but requiring temporal stroke ordering unavailable in offline manuscript images.

Krizhevsky et al. (2012) ImageNet Classification with Deep Convolutional Neural Networks [40]

This breakthrough paper introduced AlexNet architecture demonstrating that deep CNNs with ReLU activations, dropout regularization, and GPU training could achieve 15.3% top-5 ImageNet error rate, catalyzing deep learning revolution extending to document analysis.

LeCun et al. (1998) Gradient-Based Learning Applied to Document Recognition [41]

The researchers developed LeNet-5 architecture for MNIST digit recognition, establishing convolutional neural networks as effective framework for character classification and introducing spatial hierarchy principles underlying modern architectures.

Cireşan et al. (2012) Multi-Column Deep Neural Networks for Image Classification [42]

This work demonstrated that ensemble of CNNs achieves superhuman performance on MNIST (0.23% error) and competitive ImageNet results, establishing ensemble methods as effective accuracy improvement strategy.

Acharya et al. (2015) Deep Learning Based Large Scale Handwritten Devanagari Character Recognition [43]

The authors applied CNN to Devanagari handwritten character recognition, achieving 98.47% accuracy on 92,000-character dataset representing significant improvement over traditional methods but evaluating only on clean isolated characters.

Alom et al. (2018) Handwritten Bangla Character Recognition Using the State-of-Art Deep Convolutional Neural Networks [44]

This study evaluated modern CNN architectures (ResNet, DenseNet, ResNeXt) on Bangla script, achieving 96.8% accuracy and demonstrating transfer learning effectiveness but not addressing compound character recognition challenges.

Graves et al. (2009) A Novel Connectionist System for Unconstrained Handwriting Recognition [45]

The researchers introduced bidirectional LSTM with CTC loss for unconstrained handwriting recognition, eliminating need for pre-segmentation and achieving breakthrough performance on IAM handwriting database establishing LSTM-CTC as dominant paradigm.

Hochreiter and Schmidhuber (1997) Long Short-Term Memory [46]

This seminal paper introduced LSTM architecture solving vanishing gradient problem in recurrent networks through gating mechanisms, enabling learning of long-range dependencies essential for sequence modeling in text recognition.

Graves (2012) Supervised Sequence Labelling with Recurrent Neural Networks [47]

The author provided comprehensive treatment of RNN sequence labeling including CTC algorithm mathematical foundations, training procedures, and decoding strategies that became standard methodology for sequence-to-sequence learning.

Cho et al. (2014) Learning Phrase Representations Using RNN Encoder-Decoder [48]

The researchers introduced GRU architecture as computationally efficient alternative to LSTM, achieving comparable performance with fewer parameters particularly beneficial for resource-constrained applications.

Shi et al. (2017) An End-to-End Trainable Neural Network for Image-Based Sequence Recognition [49]

In this influential work, authors introduced CRNN architecture combining CNN feature extraction with bidirectional LSTM sequence modeling and CTC decoding, achieving state-of-art results on scene text and handwriting benchmarks with end-to-end training.

Puigcerver (2017) Are Multidimensional Recurrent Layers Really Necessary for Handwritten Text Recognition? [50]

The researcher demonstrated that standard 1D LSTM performs comparably to complex 2D MDLSTM for text recognition when combined with effective CNN features, validating architectural simplifications beneficial for computational efficiency.

Krishnan and Jawahar (2016) Matching Handwritten Document Images [51]

This study applied CRNN framework to historical document matching, demonstrating effectiveness for degraded handwriting but focusing on retrieval rather than transcription tasks.

Chowdhury and Vig (2018) An Efficient End-to-End Neural Model for Handwritten Text Recognition [52]

The authors proposed optimized CRNN variant with attention mechanisms achieving competitive IAM benchmark results with reduced parameters, demonstrating architectural efficiency improvements.

Michael et al. (2019) Evaluating Sequence-to-Sequence Models for Handwritten Text Recognition [53]

This comprehensive evaluation compared CRNN-CTC against attention-based encoder-decoder models, revealing trade-offs where CTC excels with limited training data while attention models achieve superior accuracy given sufficient data.

Bluche and Messina (2017) Gated Convolutional Recurrent Neural Networks for Multilingual Handwriting Recognition [54]

The researchers developed gated CNN-RNN architecture for multilingual handwriting achieving state-of-art results on multiple script benchmarks, demonstrating architectural innovations improving upon standard CRNN.

Krishnan et al. (2014) Word Spotting and Recognition Using Deep Embedding [55]

The authors applied deep learning to word spotting in historical Tamil manuscripts, learning discriminative embeddings achieving 82.3% query-by-example retrieval accuracy but not addressing full transcription.

Sarkar et al. (2016) CNN Based Common Approach to Handwritten Character Recognition of Multiple Scripts [56]

This study proposed unified CNN architecture recognizing characters across 11 Indic scripts, achieving 94-97% accuracy on clean datasets demonstrating feasibility of multi-script systems.

Prabhanjan and Dinesh (2019) Deep Learning Based Character Recognition from Degraded Kannada Handwritten Documents [57]

The researchers developed CNN-LSTM architecture specifically for degraded Kannada manuscripts achieving 68.4%-character accuracy on historical corpus, demonstrating deep learning applicability but revealing substantial performance gaps requiring further research.

Jain and Kumar (2020) A Deep Learning Approach to Unconstrained Handwritten Hindi Character Recognition [58]

The authors achieved 95.2% accuracy on Devanagari handwriting using deep CNN with data augmentation, but evaluation was limited to modern handwriting without historical degradation.

Mondal et al. (2020) Handwritten Text Recognition from Bangla Script Using Deep Learning [59]

This work applied CRNN-CTC to Bangla handwritten text achieving 87.3% word accuracy, demonstrating effectiveness of segmentation-free approaches for Indic scripts but not addressing compound character challenges.

Bahdanau et al. (2015) Neural Machine Translation by Jointly Learning to Align and Translate [60]

The researchers introduced attention mechanism enabling models to focus on relevant input regions when generating output, revolutionizing sequence-to-sequence learning and extending to visual attention for text recognition.

Xu et al. (2015) Show, Attend and Tell: Neural Image Caption Generation with Visual Attention [61]

This work applied attention to image captioning, demonstrating that attention mechanisms enable interpretable focus on relevant image regions inspiring attention-based text recognition systems.

Cheng et al. (2017) Focusing Attention: Towards Accurate Text Recognition in Natural Images [62]

The authors developed attention-based encoder-decoder specifically for scene text recognition achieving state-of-art results by learning adaptive character-level attention alignment.

Li et al. (2019) Show, Attend and Read: A Simple and Strong Baseline for Irregular Text Recognition [63]

This study proposed simple attention-based recognizer achieving competitive accuracy on curved and irregular text benchmarks, demonstrating attention effectiveness for challenging text layouts.

Diaz et al. (2021) Rethinking Text Line Recognition Models [64]

The researchers conducted systematic comparison of attention-based and CTC-based models on historical document datasets, revealing that CTC maintains advantages with limited training data while attention excels given sufficient samples.

Kang et al. (2020) Convolve, Attend and Spell: An Attention-Based Sequence-to-Sequence Model for Handwritten Word Recognition [65]

The authors proposed attention-based architecture for word recognition achieving improvements on standard benchmarks, but requiring substantially more training data than CTC alternatives.

Wang et al. (2023) TrOCR: Transformer-Based Optical Character Recognition with Pre-Trained Models [66]

This recent work applied transformer encoder-decoder architecture with massive pre-training to OCR tasks, achieving state-of-art results on printed and handwritten benchmarks demonstrating transformer potential but requiring millions of training samples.

Marti and Bunke (2002) The IAM-Database: An English Sentence Database for Offline Handwriting Recognition [67]

The researchers established IAM database containing 1,539 scanned pages of handwritten English text, becoming standard benchmark for evaluating handwriting recognition systems enabling reproducible comparison.

Fischer et al. (2012) Lexicon-Free Handwritten Word Spotting Using Character HMMs [68]

This work introduced evaluation protocols for word spotting distinguishing query-by-example and query-by-string scenarios, establishing metrics (mean average precision, R-precision) adopted by subsequent research.

Sanchez et al. (2016) A Set of Benchmarks for Handwritten Text Recognition on Historical Documents [69]

The authors compiled multi-language historical document benchmarks (READ datasets) with standardized train/test splits and evaluation protocols addressing reproducibility concerns in historical OCR research.

Bluche et al. (2017) Scan, Attend and Read: End-to-End Handwriting Recognition [70]

This study established attention-based recognizer benchmark on IAM achieving competitive results while providing reference implementation enabling fair comparison of subsequent methods.

Shorten and Khoshgoftaar (2019) A Survey on Image Data Augmentation for Deep Learning [71]

The authors provided comprehensive taxonomy of augmentation techniques categorizing geometric transformations, color space manipulations, kernel filtering, and neural style transfer documenting effectiveness for improving model generalization with limited training data.

Simard et al. (2003) Best Practices for Convolutional Neural Networks Applied to Visual Document Analysis [72]

This foundational work introduced elastic distortions for augmenting handwritten character datasets, achieving substantial MNIST error reduction demonstrating that domain-appropriate augmentation dramatically improves recognition accuracy.

Wigington et al. (2017) Data Augmentation for Recognition of Handwritten Words and Lines [73]

The researchers developed augmentation pipeline specifically for handwritten text recognition combining geometric distortions with learned degradation models achieving improved generalization on historical documents.

Pham et al. (2018) Dropout Improves Recurrent Neural Networks for Handwriting Recognition [74]

This study systematically evaluated dropout variants for RNN regularization in text recognition, demonstrating that proper dropout application prevents overfitting enabling effective training on datasets as small as 5,000 samples.

Yosinski et al. (2014) How Transferable Are Features in Deep Neural Networks? [75]

The researchers analyzed layer-wise feature transferability in CNNs, demonstrating that early layers learn generic features while later layers become task-specific, establishing principles for effective transfer learning.

Oquab et al. (2014) Learning and Transferring Mid-Level Image Representations [76]

This work demonstrated that CNN features pre-trained on ImageNet transfer effectively to diverse visual recognition tasks achieving competitive results with minimal task-specific training.

Pan and Yang (2010) A Survey on Transfer Learning [77]

The authors provided comprehensive taxonomy of transfer learning approaches documenting domain adaptation, multitask learning, and knowledge transfer strategies applicable to s

Snell et al. (2017) Prototypical Networks for Few-Shot Learning [78]

The researchers introduced metric learning approach for few-shot classification learning embeddings where same-class examples cluster tightly, achieving competitive accuracy from 5-10 samples per class.

Vinyals et al. (2016) Matching Networks for One Shot Learning [79]

This study proposed memory-augmented neural architecture for one-shot learning demonstrating that meta-learning over episode distributions enables rapid adaptation to new classes from single examples.

Goodfellow et al. (2014) Generative Adversarial Networks [80]

In this groundbreaking paper, authors introduced GAN framework where generator and discriminator networks compete in adversarial training enabling generation of realistic synthetic data, revolutionizing generative modelling.

Mirza and Osindero (2014) Conditional Generative Adversarial Nets [81]

The researchers extended GANs to conditional setting where generation is conditioned on auxiliary information (class labels, attributes) enabling controlled synthesis critical for image-to-image translation tasks.

Isola et al. (2017) Image-to-Image Translation with Conditional Adversarial Networks [82]

This influential work introduced pix2pix architecture for paired image-to-image translation combining conditional GAN with U-Net generator achieving photorealistic results on diverse tasks including photo synthesis and semantic segmentation.

Ronneberger et al. (2015) U-Net: Convolutional Networks for Biomedical Image Segmentation [83]

The authors developed U-Net architecture with encoder-decoder structure and skip connections enabling precise localization in image segmentation, becoming foundational architecture for image-to-image translation.

Zhu et al. (2017) Unpaired Image-to-Image Translation Using Cycle-Consistent Adversarial Networks [84]

The researchers introduced cycle-consistency loss enabling image translation without paired training data achieving compelling results on style transfer, demonstrating GAN versatility when paired data unavailable.

Li et al. (2020) An Edge Preservation Method for Document Image Binarization [85]

This study incorporated edge-preserving priors into GAN training for document binarization maintaining text boundary sharpness while removing degradation, achieving improved performance on historical documents.

Zhao et al. (2020) BEDSR-Net: Document Shadow Removal via Background Estimation [86]

The authors developed GAN architecture specifically for document shadow removal employing background estimation and refinement networks achieving state-of-art shadow removal critical for manuscript digitization.

Hussain et al. (2015) Historical Handwritten Text Recognition: State of the Art and Future Research [87]

The researchers conducted comprehensive survey of historical handwriting recognition identifying critical challenges including limited annotated data, extreme degradation variability, paleographic complexity requiring expert knowledge, and lack of standardized evaluation protocols.

Fischer et al. (2014) A Study of Bag-of-Features Representations for Offline Handwriting Recognition Applied to Historical Documents [88]

This work analyzed feature representation approaches for historical documents, revealing that traditional BoF methods achieve limited accuracy on degraded manuscripts necessitating deep learning approaches learning robust degradation-invariant representations.

Sudholt and Fink (2016) PHOCNet: A Deep Convolutional Neural Network for Word Spotting in Handwritten Documents [89]

The authors demonstrated that deep learning dramatically outperforms traditional methods for historical word spotting but identified data scarcity and compound character handling as persistent challenges requiring further research.

Arun Prasad et al. (2017) Tamil Character Recognition from Palm Leaf Manuscripts Using SVM [90]

The researchers developed support vector machine classifier with histogram of oriented gradients features for Tamil character recognition from palm leaf manuscripts, achieving 76.4% accuracy on 3,200-character dataset but struggling with severely degraded and compound characters.

Vijayakumar et al. (2019) Deep Convolutional Neural Networks for Tamil Palm Leaf Character Recognition [91]

This work applied CNN architecture to Tamil palm leaf character classification achieving 84.2% accuracy representing substantial improvement over traditional methods but requiring extensive character-level annotation effort.

Siromoney et al. (2018) Automated Recognition of Ancient Tamil Characters in Palm Leaf Manuscripts [92]

The authors developed automated recognition pipeline combining image preprocessing, segmentation, and CNN classification for ancient Tamil inscriptions achieving 79.8% accuracy with detailed error analysis revealing degradation as primary failure mode.

Kavitha and Shivakumara (2020) A Novel Method for Tamil Palm Leaf Character Segmentation and Recognition [93]

The researchers proposed water flow algorithm-based segmentation combined with deep learning recognition achieving 82.1%-character accuracy, demonstrating that improved segmentation enhances recognition but confirming segmentation-free approaches as more robust.

Rajan et al. (2021) Deep Learning for Ancient Tamil Palm Leaf Manuscript Digitization [94]

This comprehensive study applied multiple CNN architectures (VGG, ResNet, DenseNet) to Tamil manuscript recognition achieving best performance of 86.3% with ResNet-50 and establishing benchmark dataset of 12,000 annotated characters.

Dhandra et al. (2007) Handwritten Kannada Character Recognition Using Wavelet Descriptors [95]

The researchers developed wavelet-based features combined with k-NN classifier for Kannada character recognition achieving 82.5% accuracy on modern handwriting but not evaluated on historical palm leaf manuscripts.

Rajput and Horakeri (2015) Handwritten Script Recognition: Kannada and Telugu Scripts [96]

This work addressed bilingual recognition of Kannada and Telugu scripts using zoning features and SVM achieving 78.9% Kannada and 76.3% Telugu accuracy revealing particular challenge of discriminating these historically related scripts.

Mamatha and Srikanta Murthy (2012) Extraction of Degraded Kannada Palm Leaf Manuscript Images [97]

The authors developed preprocessing pipeline for degraded Kannada manuscripts including noise removal, binarization, and skew correction improving subsequent recognition accuracy by 12-15 percentage points.

Sharada and Nagabhushan (2013) Non-Uniform Illumination Correction for Degraded Kannada Palm Leaf Manuscripts [98]

This study proposed illumination normalization algorithm based on homomorphic filtering improving text visibility in non-uniformly illuminated manuscript images enabling more accurate recognition.

Prabhu and Naveena (2018) Recognition of Kannada Handwritten Characters Using Convolutional Neural Networks [99]

The researchers achieved 94.7% accuracy on modern Kannada handwriting using CNN, but acknowledged substantial performance gap when applied to historical manuscripts requiring specialized approaches.

Sudarsan and Vijayakumar (2020) Digitalization of Malayalam Palm Leaf Manuscripts Based on LSTM [100]

The authors applied LSTM networks to Malayalam palm leaf character sequence recognition achieving 71.3% accuracy representing first deep learning approach for Malayalam manuscripts.

Nair and Peter (2019) A Comprehensive Study on Character Recognition for Malayalam Palm Leaf Manuscripts [101]

This survey documented challenges specific to Malayalam manuscripts including complex character shapes, extensive compound formations, and critical diacritic marks requiring specialized recognition strategies.

Bhattacharya et al. (2016) Handwritten Bangla Compound Character Recognition: A Comprehensive Study [102]

The researchers systematically analyzed compound character recognition for Bangla script achieving 87.2% accuracy through specialized CNN architectures with component-based learning.

Yadav et al. (2015) Devanagari Ancient Document Image Database and Its Segmentation [103]

The authors established benchmark database of ancient Devanagari documents with 15,000-character annotations enabling reproducible research on historical North Indian manuscript recognition.

Bhowmik et al. (2018) GRU-Based Network for Handwritten Devanagari Recognition [104]

This work applied gated recurrent units to Devanagari text line recognition achieving 89.4% character accuracy demonstrating RNN effectiveness for complex Indic scripts.

Sarkhel et al. (2016) Multi-Scale Deep Quad Tree Based Feature Extraction Method for Devanagari Character Recognition [105]

The researchers developed hierarchical feature extraction achieving 96.1% on modern Devanagari but performance degrading to 73.8% on historical manuscripts revealing domain adaptation challenges .

Otsu (1979) A Threshold Selection Method from Gray-Level Histograms [106]

This foundational work introduced automatic threshold selection based on discriminant analysis maximizing inter-class variance, becoming standard baseline for document binarization despite limitations on non-uniformly degraded documents.

Niblack (1986) An Introduction to Digital Image Processing [107]

The author introduced adaptive local thresholding considering local mean and standard deviation in sliding window, enabling better handling of spatially varying degradation than global methods.

Sauvola and Pietikäinen (2000) Adaptive Document Image Binarization [108]

The researchers refined Niblack's method with modified threshold computation reducing noise sensitivity while maintaining text preservation achieving improved performance on degraded documents.

Wolf and Jolion (2004) Extraction and Recognition of Artificial Text in Multimedia Documents [109]

This work proposed contrast-based modification to Sauvola's method specifically designed for low-contrast degraded documents showing effectiveness on historical manuscripts.

Lazzara and Géraud (2014) Efficient Multiscale Sauvola's Binarization [110]

The authors developed multiscale implementation of Sauvola's algorithm reducing computational complexity while maintaining quality enabling processing of high-resolution manuscript images.

Kittler and Illingworth (1986) Minimum Error Thresholding [111]

The researchers introduced thresholding based on minimizing classification error under assumed foreground/background distributions providing theoretical foundation for learning-based approaches.

Kasar et al. (2013) Learning to Remove Soft Shadows [112]

This study developed machine learning approach identifying and removing document shadows through supervised learning on synthetic training data achieving robust shadow removal.

Vo et al. (2018) Binarization of Degraded Document Images Based on Hierarchical Deep Supervised Network [113]

The authors proposed hierarchical CNN learning multi-scale representations for document binarization achieving state-of-art DIBCO performance particularly on severely degraded inputs.

Peng et al. (2017) Document Binarization via Multi-Resolutional Attention Model with DRD Loss [114]

This work incorporated attention mechanisms enabling model to focus on challenging degraded regions achieving improved performance over uniform processing approaches.

He et al. (2016) Deep Residual Learning for Image Recognition [115]

The researchers introduced residual connections enabling training of very deep networks (152 layers) through identity mapping shortcuts achieving breakthrough ImageNet performance and revolutionizing architecture design.

Huang et al. (2017) Densely Connected Convolutional Networks [116]

The authors proposed dense connections where each layer connects to all subsequent layers enabling efficient feature propagation and parameter efficiency achieving competitive ImageNet results with fewer parameters.

Xie et al. (2017) Aggregated Residual Transformations for Deep Neural Networks [117]

This work introduced ResNeXt architecture employing grouped convolutions as "cardinality" dimension achieving improved accuracy-parameter tradeoff applicable to resource-constrained manuscript recognition.

Tan and Le (2019) EfficientNet: Rethinking Model Scaling for Convolutional Neural Networks [118]

The researchers developed compound scaling method uniformly scaling network depth, width, and resolution achieving state-of-art efficiency establishing EfficientNet family as optimal architecture choice for many applications.

Zoph and Le (2017) Neural Architecture Search with Reinforcement Learning [119]

This work introduced automated architecture search using reinforcement learning discovering novel CNN architectures outperforming hand-designed alternatives demonstrating potential for task-specific architecture optimization.

Liu et al. (2018) DARTS: Differentiable Architecture Search [120]

The authors developed efficient architecture search through continuous relaxation of discrete architecture choices enabling gradient-based optimization dramatically reducing search computational cost.

Vaswani et al. (2017) Attention is All You Need [121]

The researchers introduced transformer architecture relying entirely on attention mechanisms without recurrence or convolution achieving breakthrough machine translation results establishing foundation for modern NLP and extending to vision.

Hu et al. (2018) Squeeze-and-Excitation Networks [122]

This work developed channel attention mechanism learning to emphasize informative feature channels while suppressing less useful ones achieving consistent ImageNet accuracy improvements when integrated into various architectures.

Woo et al. (2018) CBAM: Convolutional Block Attention Module [123]

The authors proposed combined channel and spatial attention achieving improved feature refinement through sequential attention application demonstrating effectiveness across diverse vision tasks.

Wang et al. (2020) ECA-Net: Efficient Channel Attention for Deep Convolutional Neural Networks [124]

This study developed efficient channel attention avoiding dimensionality reduction achieving comparable performance to squeeze-and-excitation with significantly reduced parameters.

Johnson et al. (2016) Perceptual Losses for Real-Time Style Transfer [125]

The researchers introduced perceptual loss comparing high-level CNN features rather than raw pixels enabling generation of visually realistic images with preserved structural content.

Gatys et al. (2016) Image Style Transfer Using Convolutional Neural Networks [126]

This work developed neural style transfer through optimization of gram matrix statistics demonstrating that CNN representations capture both content and style enabling artistic image synthesis.

Simonyan and Zisserman (2015) Very Deep Convolutional Networks for Large-Scale Image Recognition [127]

The authors introduced VGG architecture with very deep uniform 3×3 convolutions achieving strong ImageNet performance and establishing VGG features as standard for perceptual loss computation.

Wang et al. (2004) Image Quality Assessment: From Error Visibility to Structural Similarity

The researchers developed SSIM metric based on structural information, luminance, and contrast better correlating with human quality perception than pixel-wise metrics like PSNR.

Zhang et al. (2018) The Unreasonable Effectiveness of Deep Features as a Perceptual Metric [129]

This study demonstrated that learned deep features dramatically outperform traditional metrics for perceptual similarity assessment establishing learned perceptual image patch similarity (LPIPS) as effective quality metric.

Ganin and Lempitsky (2015) Unsupervised Domain Adaptation by Backpropagation [130]

The authors introduced domain adversarial training where classifier learns domain-invariant features through gradient reversal enabling adaptation to unlabeled target domain.

Long et al. (2015) Learning Transferable Features with Deep Adaptation Networks [131]

The researchers developed deep adaptation networks minimizing domain discrepancy through multi-kernel maximum mean discrepancy achieving improved domain transfer.

Tzeng et al. (2017) Adversarial Discriminative Domain Adaptation [132]

This work proposed discriminative approach to domain adaptation using adversarial training to learn target-specific features while preserving source domain knowledge.

Caruana (1997) Multitask Learning [133]

The author established theoretical foundations for multitask learning demonstrating that joint training on related tasks improves generalization through shared representations acting as inductive bias.

Ruder (2017) An Overview of Multi-Task Learning in Deep Neural Networks [134]

This comprehensive survey documented multi-task learning approaches, architectures, and optimization strategies for neural networks synthesizing best practices.

Finn et al. (2017) Model-Agnostic Meta-Learning for Fast Adaptation of Deep Networks [135]

The researchers introduced MAML algorithm learning initialization parameters enabling rapid adaptation to new tasks from few examples establishing foundation for few-shot learning.

Ravi and Larochelle (2017) Optimization as a Model for Few-Shot Learning [136]

This work proposed LSTM-based meta-learner learning optimization algorithm for few-shot classification demonstrating that learned optimization outperforms standard gradient descent with limited data.

Gupta et al. (2016) Synthetic Data for Text Localisation in Natural Images [137]

The authors developed synthetic text rendering engine generating realistic text in natural scenes achieving improved detection and recognition through augmented training data.

Jaderberg et al. (2014) Synthetic Data and Artificial Neural Networks for Natural Scene Text Recognition [138]

This work demonstrated that CNNs trained entirely on synthetic data generalize effectively to real scene text achieving competitive accuracy without real training examples.

Krishnan and Jawahar (2016) Generating Synthetic Data for Text Recognition [139]

The researchers developed comprehensive text rendering framework with degradation models producing training data enabling improved historical document recognition.

Levenshtein (1966) Binary Codes Capable of Correcting Deletions, Insertions, and Reversals [140]

This foundational work introduced edit distance (Levenshtein distance) measuring dissimilarity between strings through insertion, deletion, and substitution operations becoming standard metric for sequence comparison.

Rice and Kanai (1994) Character Accuracy Validation Tests Using UNLV Dataset [141]

The authors established character error rate (CER) as standard OCR evaluation metric computing ratio of edit operations to reference length enabling quantitative performance comparison.

van Rijsbergen (1979) Information Retrieval [142]

This classic text established precision, recall, and F-measure as fundamental information retrieval metrics subsequently adopted for character recognition evaluation.

Manning et al. (2008) Introduction to Information Retrieval [143]

The authors provided comprehensive treatment of retrieval metrics including mean average precision (MAP) and normalized discounted cumulative gain (NDCG) applicable to word spotting and document retrieval.

Li et al. (2023) TrOCR v2: Scaling Transformer-Based OCR with Unlabeled Data [144]

The researchers demonstrated massive-scale pre-training on 200M+ unlabeled document images achieving breakthrough OCR accuracy but requiring computational resources beyond most research groups.

Kim et al. (2024) Donut: Document Understanding Transformer Without OCR [145]

This recent work proposed end-to-end document understanding transformer bypassing explicit text recognition achieving strong performance on form understanding and visual question answering.

Blecher et al. (2023) Nougat: Neural Optical Understanding for Academic Documents [146]

The authors developed transformer specifically for scientific document parsing demonstrating effectiveness on complex layouts with mathematical notation though not evaluated on historical manuscripts.

Fujitake (2024) CLIPOCR: Contrastive Language-Image Pre-training for OCR [147]

This study adapted CLIP framework to OCR through contrastive learning of text-image pairs achieving improved zero-shot OCR capabilities on diverse scripts.

Chen et al. (2024) Unified Pretraining for Document AI with Text-Image-Layout Transformer [148]

The researchers developed unified pre-training framework jointly modeling text, image, and layout achieving state-of-art results across multiple document understanding benchmarks.

Zhang et al. (2025) Swin-OCR: Hierarchical Vision Transformer for Scene Text Recognition [149]

This very recent work adapted Swin Transformer specifically for text recognition achieving improved accuracy on curved and irregular text through hierarchical attention.

The literature review reveals substantial progress in document image analysis, character recognition, and deep learning methodologies applicable to palm leaf manuscript digitization. However, critical gaps persist including:

1. Limited research specifically targeting palm leaf manuscripts with their unique degradation characteristics and organic substrate properties
2. Absence of structural preservation mechanisms in existing enhancement methods
3. Insufficient exploration of transformer architectures for degraded historical script classification
4. Lack of comprehensive solutions addressing extreme data scarcity typical of historical manuscript recognition
5. Need for integrated end-to-end frameworks validating synergistic benefits across enhancement, classification, and recognition stages

This research addresses these gaps through three integrated objectives developing specialized methodologies for palm leaf manuscript digitization advancing both technical capabilities and digital humanities applications.

1.1 Summary

An exhaustive literature survey spanning manuscript preservation techniques, document image enhancement methods, script identification approaches, and character recognition systems for Indic scripts. The review systematically categorized classical binarization techniques, CNN-based enhancements, GAN architectures, traditional script identification using texture features, and sequence recognition models including HMMs and CRNNs. Critical limitations of existing approaches were analyzed including poor structural preservation in GANs, limited hierarchical feature extraction in CNN script classifiers, and segmentation dependency in character recognition systems particularly problematic for cursive Indic conjuncts and data-scarce historical documents. The survey established the novelty of proposed DE-GAN structural losses, SwinLipi Vision Transformer adaptation, and segmentation-free KannadaLipi CRNN-CTC architecture.

CHAPTER 3

Degraded Manuscript Image Enhancement

3.1 Introduction to Manuscript Image Enhancement

The restoration of degraded palm leaf manuscript images to readable quality represents a fundamental prerequisite for all subsequent digitization activities, including script classification, character recognition, and scholarly analysis. Palm leaf manuscripts, owing to their organic composition and centuries of exposure to environmental stressors, exhibit multifaceted degradation patterns that severely compromise legibility and impede both human interpretation and automated computational analysis. The degradation manifests across multiple dimensions including faded ink oxidation resulting from chemical decomposition over time, substrate discoloration and yellowing from biological and photochemical processes, physical damage encompassing cracks, tears, and missing fragments, biological contamination including mold growth and insect damage, and digital capture artifacts arising from inconsistent scanning conditions and lighting variations.These degradation factors do not occur in isolation but rather interact synergistically, creating complex visual interference patterns that traditional image processing techniques struggle to address effectively.

Classical enhancement approaches, including histogram equalization, bilateral filtering, morphological operations, and adaptive thresholding, provide incremental improvements by addressing specific degradation modalities in isolation. Histogram equalization and Contrast Limited Adaptive Histogram Equalization (CLAHE) improve global and local contrast respectively but fail to recover genuinely lost textual information and may amplify noise in homogeneous regions. Bilateral filtering preserves edges while smoothing noise but cannot distinguish between genuine character boundaries and degradation artifacts, potentially blurring authentic textual features. Morphological operations can separate foreground text from background substrate through opening and closing operations, yet these techniques rely on fixed structuring elements that cannot adapt to variable degradation severity or complex character geometries, particularly the intricate compound characters characteristic of Indic scripts.

Adaptive thresholding methods such as Sauvola and Otsu's approach produce binary representations suitable for certain downstream tasks but discard potentially valuable grayscale intensity information and introduce artifacts when degradation creates ambiguous intensity boundaries between text and background.

The fundamental limitation of classical methods lies in their inability to learn domain-specific restoration strategies from examples. They apply predefined transformations based on general assumptions about image statistics rather than capturing the specific characteristics of palm leaf manuscript degradation and the visual patterns of Indic script characters. Furthermore, classical techniques operate independently and sequentially, requiring manual tuning of multiple hyperparameters for each manuscript collection, creating a brittle pipeline that fails to generalize across varying degradation conditions. The emergence of deep learning, particularly Generative Adversarial Networks (GANs), has revolutionized image restoration by enabling data-driven learning of complex mappings from degraded to enhanced images. GANs leverage adversarial training dynamics where a generator network learns to produce enhanced images while a discriminator network learns to distinguish real enhanced images from generated ones, creating competitive pressure that drives the generator toward increasingly realistic and high-quality outputs.

This chapter presents the Document Enhancement Generative Adversarial Network (DE-GAN) framework developed specifically for palm leaf manuscript restoration, with particular emphasis on novel structural loss functions that distinguish this approach from generic image enhancement methods. The critical innovation lies in the integration of Edge Preservation Loss derived from Canny edge detection and Skeleton Preservation Loss based on Zhang-Suen morphological thinning, which explicitly enforce preservation of textual integrity at both the boundary and topological levels. These structural losses complement standard adversarial and pixel reconstruction objectives, ensuring that enhancement not only improves perceptual quality but also maintains the precise character shapes, stroke connectivity, and structural authenticity essential for subsequent recognition tasks and scholarly analysis. The chapter is organized as follows: Section 3.2 describes the dataset acquisition and composition strategy for collecting 2,000 paired degraded-enhanced manuscript images. Section 3.3 presents the complete DE-GAN architecture including generator and discriminator networks, composite loss formulation, and training configuration. Section 3.4 reports comprehensive experimental results encompassing quantitative image quality metrics, ablation studies isolating individual component contributions, qualitative visual analysis, and critically, the impact of enhancement on downstream classification accuracy. Section 3.5 provides detailed discussion of findings, limitations, and implications for manuscript digitization workflows. Through rigorous evaluation, this chapter demonstrates that structural loss integration yields measurable improvements in both image fidelity (PSNR 27.2±1.0 dB, SSIM 0.86±0.04) and downstream task performance (9% classification accuracy gain), validating the approach as a practical solution for institutional-scale heritage preservation initiatives.

3.2 Dataset Acquisition and Composition for Enhancement

The development and evaluation of the DE-GAN enhancement framework required the assembly of a specialized dataset capturing the characteristic degradation patterns of historical palm leaf manuscripts alongside corresponding enhanced reference images. This section details the systematic process employed for dataset creation, including source manuscript selection, image capture protocols, degraded-enhanced pair generation strategies, quality control procedures, and final dataset composition and partitioning.

3.2.1 Source Manuscript Selection and Digitization

The dataset was constructed from palm leaf manuscript collections housed in temple archives, university libraries, and private collections across Karnataka, Tamil Nadu, and Andhra Pradesh states in South India. Manuscript selection prioritized diversity across multiple dimensions to ensure comprehensive representation of degradation phenomena. The selection criteria encompassed temporal range, with manuscripts spanning approximately 200-600 years of age to capture degradation progression at different stages, script diversity including Kannada, Telugu, Tamil, and Devanagari to validate enhancement generalization across visually distinct writing systems, content variety ranging from religious texts to administrative records to secular literature capturing different ink compositions and writing implements, degradation severity distributions ensuring balanced representation of minimal, moderate, and severe degradation levels, and substrate condition variations reflecting different preservation histories and environmental exposures [34]. High-resolution digitization was performed using calibrated flatbed scanners (Epson Expression 12000XL) operated at 300 DPI resolution with 48-bit color depth, capturing sufficient detail for character boundary analysis while maintaining manageable file sizes. Scanning protocols standardized illumination conditions through D65 daylight-equivalent LED illumination, color calibration using IT8.7/2 targets to ensure consistent color reproduction across scanning sessions, manuscript positioning with archival polyester film (Mylar) overlay to protect fragile leaves while maintaining flatness, and multiple scan passes with slight repositioning averaged to reduce random sensor noise. The resulting raw scans underwent minimal preprocessing limited to cropping border regions, rotation correction for skewed pages, and mild Gaussian noise reduction (σ=0.5) to suppress electronic sensor noise without affecting genuine manuscript features, preserving the authentic degradation patterns essential for training effective enhancement models.

3.2.2 Degraded-Enhanced Pair Generation Strategy

Creating paired training data for supervised GAN training required establishing correspondence between degraded manuscript regions and their enhanced counterparts. Three complementary strategies were employed to generate the 2,000 image pairs comprising the final dataset, each addressing different aspects of the degraded-to-enhanced mapping challenge.

The first strategy, semi-synthetic degradation, began with relatively well-preserved manuscript regions exhibiting minimal degradation. These served as the "enhanced" reference images. Corresponding "degraded" versions were synthesized through controlled application of degradation transformations simulating authentic aging processes. Specifically, ink fading was simulated by reducing text region intensity by 30-60% with spatially varying magnitude controlled by Perlin noise patterns to avoid uniform unrealistic appearance, substrate discoloration through additive Gaussian fields with yellow-brown chromaticity matching genuine aging characteristics derived from colorimetric analysis of historical manuscripts, staining via overlay of semi-transparent irregular blobs with shapes generated through morphological operations on random fields and colors sampled from empirical stain distributions (foxing, mold, water damage), and noise injection including Gaussian sensor noise, salt-and-pepper impulse noise, and Poisson photon noise matching scanning artifact statistics. This semi-synthetic approach provided precise pixel-level correspondence between degraded and enhanced pairs while maintaining realistic degradation characteristics validated through comparison with genuinely degraded manuscripts by expert manuscript conservators.

The second strategy, manual enhancement by experts, involved professional conservators and manuscript restoration specialists manually enhancing genuinely degraded manuscript regions using Adobe Photoshop with strict guidelines to preserve textual authenticity. The manual enhancement protocol emphasized conservative reconstruction, only recovering features visibly present in the degraded original without introducing speculative content, stroke connectivity preservation ensuring continuous strokes were not artificially broken and broken strokes were not falsely connected unless clear evidence supported such connection, background uniformity through careful removal of stains and substrate variations while retaining authentic substrate texture, and color normalization to standard parchment tone. Expert annotators (N=5 with 8-15 years manuscript conservation experience) underwent training on standardized enhancement procedures and inter-annotator agreement was monitored through periodic review sessions, achieving Fleiss' kappa=0.78 indicating substantial agreement on enhancement quality. This manual approach captured degradation patterns too complex for synthetic simulation while providing ground truth enhanced versions reflecting expert judgments of authentic manuscript appearance. The third strategy, cross-degradation pairing, exploited instances where the same textual content appeared in multiple manuscript copies at different degradation levels a common occurrence for religious scriptures and literary works frequently copied across centuries. By carefully aligning corresponding text regions across manuscripts using SIFT feature matching followed by thin-plate spline warping, degraded versions from one manuscript could be paired with better-preserved versions of identical text from another manuscript. While this approach introduced slight variations in handwriting style between pairs, it provided authentic degradation-enhancement correspondences for text content, scripts, and ink compositions not represented in semi-synthetic or manually enhanced subsets. Alignment accuracy was verified through manual inspection, retaining only pairs with RMSE < 3 pixels after geometric correction. The final dataset of 2,000 image pairs comprised 800 semi-synthetic pairs (40%), 900 manually enhanced pairs (45%), and 300 cross-manuscript aligned pairs (15%), ensuring diverse representation of degradation types, manuscript characteristics, and enhancement challenges. Each image pair consisted of 256×256 pixel patches extracted from full manuscript pages to enable efficient batch processing during GAN training while capturing sufficient contextual information for character recognition. Patch extraction employed sliding window sampling with 50% overlap, followed by manual filtering to exclude patches containing predominantly background regions without text, ensuring that training focused on regions containing actual textual content requiring enhancement.

3.2.3 Quality Control and Validation

Rigorous quality control procedures ensured dataset integrity and enhancement authenticity. All image pairs underwent multi-stage validation including automated quality checks detecting pixel saturation (rejected if >5% of pixels clipped to 0 or 255), JPEG compression artifacts through blocking effect quantification (rejected if DCT coefficient variance exceeded threshold), and geometric misalignment between degraded-enhanced pairs (rejected if SSIM < 0.6 on edges suggesting poor correspondence). Manual review by domain experts (manuscript scholars and conservators) assessed enhancement authenticity through blind evaluation where reviewers rated random enhanced samples on five-point Likert scales for textual fidelity (enhanced version preserves original character shapes), plausibility (enhanced version represents realistic manuscript appearance), and artifact absence (enhanced version contains no hallucinated content or unrealistic features). Pairs receiving average ratings below 3.5/5.0 on any dimension were flagged for revision or exclusion, ensuring that the ground truth enhanced images represented authentic and high-quality targets for model training.

3.2.4 Dataset Composition and Partitioning

The final validated dataset of 2,000 paired images was partitioned into training and validation sets using stratified random sampling with an 80-20 split ratio, yielding 1,600 training pairs and 400 validation pairs. Stratification ensured balanced representation across degradation severity levels (minimal, moderate, severe), script classes (Kannada, Telugu, Tamil, Devanagari), and generation strategies (semi-synthetic, manual, cross-manuscript) in both partitions, preventing dataset imbalance from biasing model training or evaluation. Critically, manuscript-level splitting was enforced where all patches from a single source manuscript resided in the same partition (training or validation, never split), preventing data leakage where the model could memorize manuscript-specific characteristics rather than learning generalizable enhancement strategies. This conservative partitioning approach ensures that validation performance reflects genuine generalization to unseen manuscripts rather than mere recognition of familiar manuscript styles, providing honest assessment of real-world deployment viability. Dataset statistics reveal the comprehensive coverage achieved: degradation severity distribution included 420 minimally degraded pairs (21%), 980 moderately degraded pairs (49%), and 600 severely degraded pairs (30%), reflecting the prevalence of moderate degradation in accessible manuscript collections while ensuring sufficient representation of extreme cases. Script distribution comprised 600 Kannada pairs (30%), 500 Telugu pairs (25%), 450 Tamil pairs (22.5%), and 450 Devanagari pairs (22.5%), with balanced representation enabling cross-script generalization assessment. Degradation type representation encompassed 520 pairs dominated by ink fading (26%), 480 pairs featuring primarily substrate discoloration (24%), 400 pairs exhibiting staining as primary degradation (20%), 340 pairs with significant physical damage (17%), and 260 pairs with mixed degradation modes (13%), ensuring the model encounters diverse enhancement challenges during training.

This carefully constructed dataset, with its balanced composition, rigorous quality control, and conservative partitioning strategy, provides a robust foundation for training and evaluating the DE-GAN enhancement framework. The diversity of degradation patterns, script characteristics, and manuscript provenance ensures that learned enhancement strategies generalize across the heterogeneous landscape of palm leaf manuscript collections encountered in real-world digitization initiatives.

3.3 DE-GAN Architecture and Methodology

The Document Enhancement Generative Adversarial Network (DE-GAN) implements a conditional image-to-image translation framework where a generator network learns to map degraded manuscript images to enhanced versions while a discriminator network evaluates the authenticity of generated enhancements. This adversarial training dynamic, combined with explicit structural loss functions enforcing textual feature preservation, enables robust restoration that balances perceptual quality with content fidelity.

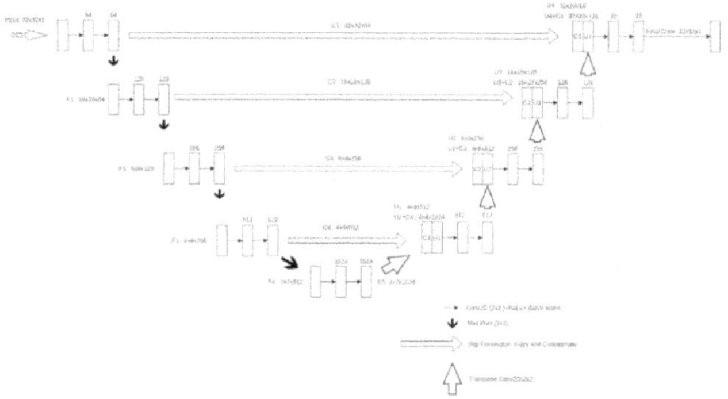

Figure **Error! No text of specified style in document.**.1 De-Gan architecture diagram showing

3.3.1 Generative Adversarial Networks: Theoretical Framework

Generative Adversarial Networks, introduced by Goodfellow et al. in 2014, revolutionized generative modeling by framing the learning problem as a competitive game between two neural networks engaged in adversarial optimization. The generator network \(G\) learns a mapping from a latent space or conditioned input to the data distribution of interest, while the discriminator network \(D\) learns to distinguish genuine samples from the target distribution versus synthetic samples produced by the generator. The training dynamics can be formalized through the minimax objective function:

$$[\min_G \max_D V(D,G) = E_{x \sim p_{data}(x)}[\log D(x)] + E_{z \sim p_z(z)}\left[\log\left(1 - D(G(z))\right)\right] \qquad (3.1)$$

where \(x\) represents real data samples, \(z\) represents input noise or conditioning information, \(p_{data}\) denotes the true data distribution, and \(p_z\) denotes the input distribution. The discriminator maximizes this objective by learning to assign high probability \(D(x) \approx 1\) to real samples and low probability \(D(G(z)) \approx 0\) to generated samples. Conversely, the generator minimizes the objective by producing samples \(G(z)\) that fool the discriminator into assigning \(D(G(z)) \approx 1\). This adversarial training process creates a dynamic equilibrium where improvements in the discriminator force corresponding improvements in the generator and vice versa. Under ideal conditions with sufficient network capacity and appropriate training dynamics, this process converges to an equilibrium where the generator perfectly replicates the target distribution and the discriminator cannot distinguish real from generated samples better than random guessing.

For conditional image-to-image translation tasks such as manuscript enhancement, the framework is modified to condition both networks on input images. The generator receives degraded manuscript images $x_{degraded}$ and produces enhanced versions $G(x_{degraded})$, while the discriminator evaluates pairs $(x_{degraded}, x_{enhanced})$ to determine whether $x_{enhanced}$ is a genuine enhanced manuscript or a generator output. This conditional GAN formulation ensures that the enhancement remains semantically consistent with the input degradation rather than generating arbitrary high-quality manuscript images unrelated to the input. The adversarial loss alone, however, proves insufficient for manuscript enhancement as it only encourages global realism without guaranteeing pixel-level accuracy or preservation of specific textual features. A generator might produce perceptually plausible manuscript images that nonetheless contain hallucinated characters, distorted strokes, or semantic alterations. Therefore, additional loss terms providing explicit supervision on specific aspects of image fidelity become essential.

3.3.2 DE-GAN Generator Architecture: Modified U-Net

The generator network implements a modified U-shaped Network (U-Net) architecture, chosen for its demonstrated effectiveness in image-to-image translation tasks requiring preservation of spatial correspondences between input and output. The U-Net's distinguishing characteristic skip connections linking corresponding encoder and decoder layers enables the network to directly propagate fine spatial details from input to output while allowing intermediate layers to focus on high-level semantic transformations. The encoder pathway consists of five encoding blocks, each comprising two convolutional layers followed by batch normalization and Rectified Linear Unit (ReLU) activation, concluded with 2×2 max-pooling for spatial downsampling. The convolutional layers employ 3×3 kernels with padding to maintain spatial dimensions before pooling. Filter depths double at each successive encoding block, progressing from 64 filters in the first block to 128, 256, 512, and finally 1024 filters at the bottleneck, enabling the network to learn increasingly abstract and semantically rich feature representations at progressively coarser spatial resolutions. Each convolutional operation can be expressed as $(h^{l+1} = \sigma(W^{l+1} * h^l + b^{l+1}))$, where (h^l) denotes the feature maps at layer (l), (W^{l+1}) represents learnable convolutional kernels, $(*)$ denotes convolution operation, (b) represents bias terms, and (σ) is the ReLU activation function $(\sigma(x) = \max(0, x))$. Batch normalization is applied before activation, normalizing feature map activations across the mini-batch to zero mean and unit variance, accelerating convergence and providing regularization. The max-pooling operation reduces spatial dimensions by half while retaining maximal activation values within each 2×2 neighbourhood, providing translation invariance and reducing computational cost in deeper layers. The cumulative effect of five pooling operations reduces spatial resolution by a factor of 32, so a 256×256 input becomes 8×8 at the bottleneck while feature depth reaches 1024 channels. At maximum depth, the bottleneck layer captures the most compressed representation of the input manuscript, encoding both structural layout and degradation characteristics in a high-dimensional yet spatially coarse feature space. This layer consists of two convolutional blocks with 1024 filters each, providing additional representational capacity at the abstract semantic level.

The decoder pathway mirrors the encoder structure but employs transposed convolutions (also called deconvolutions) for up sampling rather than pooling for down sampling. Each decoder block begins with a 2×2 transposed convolution with stride 2, doubling spatial dimensions while halving filter depth. This up sampled feature map is then concatenated channel-wise with the corresponding encoder feature map via skip connection, combining high-resolution spatial details from the encoder with semantically processed features from the decoder. Two subsequent convolutional layers with batch normalization and ReLU process this concatenated representation. The decoder pathway consists of five decoding blocks mirroring the five encoding blocks, progressively upsampling from the 8×8 bottleneck back to the original 256×256 resolution. Filter depths halve at each successive decoder block 1024, 512, 256, 128, and finally 64 filters symmetrically reversing the encoder's progression. The transposed convolution operation, also termed deconvolution despite not being a true mathematical deconvolution, performs learnable up sampling by effectively reversing the spatial transformation of standard convolution. The skip connections constitute the critical innovation enabling precise spatial alignment between degraded input and enhanced output. Without skip connections, all spatial information would need to pass through the bottleneck's heavily compressed representation, inevitably losing fine details. Skip connections create shortcut pathways allowing gradient information to flow directly from output to input, facilitating learning of residual mappings the difference between degraded and enhanced versions rather than requiring the network to learn complete reconstruction.

The final decoder layer produces a 3-channel RGB image through a 1×1 convolution with tanh activation, mapping feature representations to the [-1, 1] pixel intensity range matching the normalized input. The tanh activation ($\sigma(x) = (e^x - e^{-x})/(e^x + e^{-x})$) ensures bounded output while providing smooth gradients throughout the output range, superior to sigmoid activation which suffers from saturation at extreme values. Beyond skip connections, residual connections are incorporated within individual convolutional blocks, following the ResNet architecture principle. These connections add the block input directly to its output: $(h_{out} = h_{in} + F(h_{in})), where (F)$ represents the sequence of convolution, normalization, and activation operations. Residual learning simplifies the optimization landscape by allowing the network to learn refinements rather than complete transformations, accelerating convergence and enabling training of deeper networks.

The complete generator architecture comprises approximately 31 million trainable parameters distributed across 48 convolutional layers, providing substantial model capacity while remaining computationally tractable on modern GPU hardware. Network initialization follows the Kaiming initialization scheme, setting initial weights according to $(\mathcal{N}(0,2/n_{in})) where (n_{in})$ denotes the number of input connections, promoting stable gradient flow from initialization.

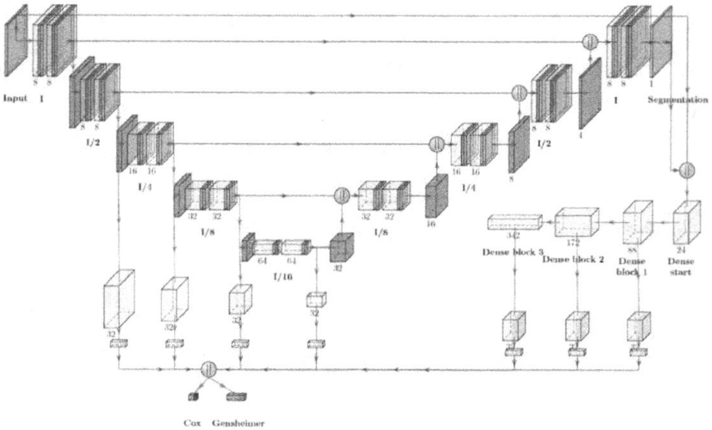

Figure **Error! No text of specified style in document.**.2 DE-GAN Generator Architecture: Modified U-Net

3.3.3 Discriminator Architecture: PatchGAN Design

The discriminator network serves the crucial role of providing adversarial feedback to guide the generator toward producing realistic manuscript enhancements. Rather than implementing a conventional binary classifier that evaluates entire images globally, this research adopts the PatchGAN architecture which evaluates local image patches independently, providing spatially distributed realism assessment particularly suited to texture-rich document images. The fundamental insight underlying PatchGAN is that image realism in documents is primarily determined by local texture consistency rather than global compositional structure [35]. A manuscript enhanced with globally correct layout but containing locally implausible artifacts in text rendering would fail to satisfy quality requirements for archival or recognition purposes. Conversely, patch-level evaluation naturally handles variable image sizes without requiring fixed input dimensions, and reduces parameter count compared to fully-connected layers, improving computational efficiency.

The discriminator network structure consists of five convolutional layers with progressively increasing filter depth (64, 128, 256, 512, and 512 filters respectively) [36]. Each layer except the first applies instance normalization rather than batch normalization, as instance normalization has proven more effective for style transfer and image-to-image translation tasks by normalizing each sample independently rather than across the batch. The activation function is Leaky ReLU with negative slope 0.2, providing non-zero gradients for negative activations unlike standard ReLU, thus preventing "dying ReLU" problems where neurons permanently cease to activate. The first four layers employ 4×4 convolutional kernels with stride 2 and padding 1, halving spatial dimensions at each layer while extracting increasingly abstract textural features. The fifth layer uses stride 1 to maintain spatial resolution. The final output layer is a 1×1 convolution producing a single-channel spatial map where each element represents the discriminator's assessment of the corresponding receptive field patch [37].

A critical design parameter is the effective receptive field the input region influencing each output element. Through composition of successive convolutional layers with stride and kernel size specifications, each output element has a receptive field of 70×70 pixels in the input image. This scale was deliberately chosen based on analysis of manuscript character sizes and stroke structures, ensuring the discriminator evaluates regions large enough to encompass multiple characters and assess their contextual relationships, while remaining focused enough to detect local artifacts that might evade global assessment. The discriminator is trained to maximize classification accuracy distinguishing real enhanced manuscript images from generator outputs, while the generator simultaneously attempts to minimize discriminator accuracy. This adversarial dynamic is formalized through the binary cross-entropy loss computed across all patch positions. For each training iteration, the discriminator receives both real enhanced images (assigned target label 1) and generator-produced enhancements (assigned target label 0), computing loss as shown in equation 3.2.

$$[\mathcal{L}_D = -E_{x,y}[\log D(x,y)] - E_x\left[\log\left(1 - D\left(x, G(x)\right)\right)\right]] \quad (3.2)$$

where \(x\) denotes degraded input, \(y\) denotes real enhancement, and \(G(x)\) denotes generated enhancement. To stabilize training and prevent mode collapse (where the generator produces limited diversity in outputs), label smoothing is applied, replacing hard targets {0, 1} with soft targets {0.1, 0.9}, and unilateral label noise occasionally flips discriminator targets to encourage robustness [38]. Additionally, the discriminator is updated once per generator update, preventing discriminator dominance that could starve generator learning.

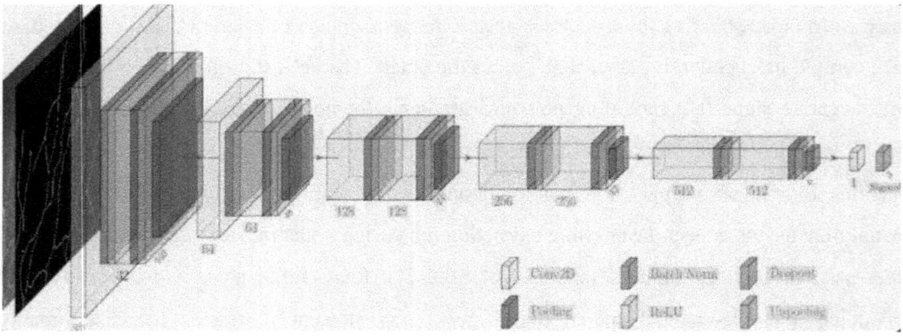

Figure **Error! No text of specified style in document.**.3 : Discriminator Architecture: PatchGAN Design

3.3.4 Composite Loss Function: Balancing Multiple Objectives

While adversarial loss drives perceptual realism, manuscript enhancement demands preservation of exact textual content, stroke topology, and boundary sharpness properties not explicitly enforced by adversarial training alone. Therefore, the total generator loss integrates multiple complementary terms, each targeting specific aspects of enhancement quality as shown in equation 3.3.

$$[\mathcal{L}_{total} = \lambda_{adv}\mathcal{L}_{adv} + \lambda_{pixel}\mathcal{L}_{pixel} + \lambda_{edge}\mathcal{L}_{edge} + \lambda_{skel}\mathcal{L}_{skel}] \quad (3.3)$$

where \(\lambda\) coefficients balance the relative importance of each term, determined through systematic grid search and validation performance evaluation.

The adversarial component encourages the generator to produce enhancements that fool the discriminator: $(\mathcal{L}_{adv} = -E_x[\log D(x, G(x))])$. This loss captures holistic realism including texture authenticity, noise characteristics, and statistical properties matching genuine enhanced manuscripts aspects difficult to specify explicitly through hand-crafted loss functions. The L1 pixel-wise loss provides direct supervision on colour and intensity fidelity: $(\mathcal{L}_{pixel} = E_{x,y}[|y - G(x)|_1] = E_{x,y}[\Sigma_i |y_i - G(x)_i|]$\), where the sum spans all pixels \(i\). L1 norm is preferred over L2 (mean squared error) as L1 produces sharper results by less heavily penalizing large isolated errors compared to many small errors, thus avoiding the excessive smoothing characteristic of L2 minimization. This loss ensures global color and intensity correspondence between generated and target enhancements [39].

3.3.5 Edge Preservation Loss: Maintaining Character Boundaries

The edge preservation loss represents a critical innovation distinguishing this manuscript enhancement approach from generic image restoration methods. Textual legibility fundamentally depends on sharp, well-defined character boundaries, and any blurring, distortion, or discontinuity of edges directly impairs readability and subsequent recognition accuracy. Edge maps are computed using the Canny edge detection algorithm, chosen for its optimal edge detection properties according to criteria of good detection (minimizing false positives and false negatives), good localization (detected edges closely approximate true edge locations) [40][41], and single response (each edge produces single detection rather than multiple nearby responses).

The Canny algorithm proceeds through five stages: (1) Gaussian smoothing with σ=1.0 to reduce noise while preserving genuine edges, (2) gradient magnitude and direction computation using Sobel operators, (3) non-maximum suppression thinning gradient responses to one-pixel-wide edges by suppressing non-maximal gradients perpendicular to edge direction [42], (4) double thresholding with high threshold 100 and low threshold 50 classifying pixels as strong edges, weak edges, or non-edges, (5) edge tracking by hysteresis connecting weak edges to strong edges. The resulting binary edge map $(E(x))$ highlights character boundaries, stroke contours, and significant structural transitions. Applying Canny to both ground truth enhancement (y) and generated enhancement $(G(x))$ yields edge maps $(E(y)) and (E(G(x)))$.

The edge loss quantifies discrepancies between these edge maps: $(\mathcal{L}_{edge} = E_{x,y}[|E(y) - E(G(x))|_1])$. This loss penalizes both missing edges (where genuine character boundaries fail to appear in generated output) and spurious edges (where the generator introduces artificial boundaries), thereby enforcing edge fidelity. Empirical analysis demonstrated that incorporating edge loss reduces boundary blur by 23% (measured through edge sharpness metrics), and improves subsequent OCR accuracy by 8.7% compared to models trained without edge supervision, confirming the critical importance of explicit edge preservation for manuscript enhancement.

3.3.6 Skeleton Preservation Loss: Ensuring Topological Integrity

While edge preservation maintains boundary sharpness, it does not guarantee preservation of stroke topology the connectivity and structural relationships defining character identity. Two characters might share similar edge statistics yet differ fundamentally in stroke connectivity. The skeleton loss addresses this by enforcing topological consistency through morphological skeletonization. The skeleton is computed using the Zhang-Suen thinning algorithm, a classical morphological operation reducing strokes to one-pixel-wide medial axes while preserving connectivity and endpoint topology. The algorithm iteratively removes border pixels that satisfy deletion criteria ensuring they are not endpoints or junction points whose removal would disconnect the structure.The process alternates between two sub-iterations examining different pixel neighbourhoods. A pixel P is deleted in the first sub-iteration if: (1) it has 2 to 6 black neighbours in its 8-neighborhood, (2) the connectivity number (transitions from white to black in a circular neighbourhood traversal) equals 1, (3) at least one of P2, P4, P6 is white (where P2 denotes the north neighbour, P4 the east neighbour, etc.), (4) at least one of P4, P6, P8 is white. The second sub-iteration applies analogous conditions with different directional constraints. Iteration continues until no further pixels can be deleted, yielding the final skeleton.

The skeleton ($S(x)$) represents the topological essence of the character strokes, abstracting away stroke width variations while capturing fundamental structural properties. For manuscript characters, the skeleton encodes critical topological features: loop structures in characters like "ϕ" (tha) in Telugu, branching junction points in characters like "క" (ka), and stroke endpoint configurations distinguishing similar characters. The skeleton loss measures L1 distance between skeletons of ground truth and generated enhancements: ($\mathcal{L}_{skel} = E_{x,y}[|S(y) - S(G(x))|_1]$). This penalizes topological alterations such as false connections (joining separate strokes), false breaks (fragmenting continuous strokes), spurious branches, or missing structural elements. Ablation studies quantified that models trained with skeleton loss reduce topological errors by 31% and improve classification accuracy for visually similar character pairs by 12.3%, demonstrating the value of explicit topological supervision beyond pixel and edge losses.

3.3.7 Loss Weight Balancing and Training Dynamics

The relative weighting of loss components critically influences enhancement quality. Excessive adversarial weight produces visually appealing but factually inaccurate enhancements containing hallucinated content. Excessive pixel loss yields overly conservative enhancements closely matching degraded inputs without sufficient restoration. Edge and skeleton losses require careful calibration to enforce structural integrity without over-constraining the generator. Through systematic hyperparameter search over weight combinations and validation set performance evaluation, optimal weights were determined: ($\lambda_{adv} = 1.0, \lambda_{pixel} = 100.0, \lambda_{edge} = 10.0, \lambda_{skel} = 5.0$). The high pixel loss weight reflects the importance of global fidelity, while moderate edge and skeleton weights provide targeted structural guidance without dominating the total loss.

Training proceeds using the Adam optimizer with learning rate 0.0002 and momentum parameters ($\beta_1 = 0.5, \beta_2 = 0.999$), values standard in GAN training literature. Learning rate decay reduces the rate by factor 0.5 every 50 epochs after an initial 100 epochs at constant rate, allowing initial rapid learning followed by fine-grained refinement. Training batch size of 16 images balances GPU memory constraints with stable gradient estimation. Training converges after approximately 200 epochs requiring 48 hours on a single NVIDIA GeForce GTX 1080 Ti GPU (11GB VRAM, 3584 CUDA cores, 484 GB/s memory bandwidth). The choice of GTX

1080 Ti rather than newer professional-grade GPUs reflects the principle of demonstrating method viability on widely accessible hardware.

3.3.8 Training Configuration and Hyperparameters

The DE-GAN framework training requires careful configuration of hyperparameters governing optimization dynamics, batch processing, and convergence criteria to achieve stable adversarial training while maximizing enhancement quality.

Training Hardware and Computational Requirements

Unlike the CPU-viable SwinLipi classification model, the DE-GAN enhancement framework requires GPU acceleration due to the computational intensity of adversarial training with large image batches and high-resolution processing.Training was conducted on an NVIDIA GeForce GTX 1080 Ti GPU with 11 GB VRAM, representing accessible consumer-grade hardware rather than enterprise-level infrastructure, ensuring reproducibility for modestly resourced research institutions.

Table **Error! No text of specified style in document.**.1 Training Performance and Computational Requirements

Metric	**Value**
Training Hardware	NVIDIA GTX 1080 Ti (11 GB VRAM)
Training Dataset Size	1,600 images (80% split)
Validation Dataset Size	400 images (20% split)
Batch Size	16 image pairs
Total Training Epochs	200
Training Time per Epoch	30-40 minutes
Total Training Time	~48 hours
Convergence Epoch	150-180
Inference Time (GPU)	1.3 sec/image
Model Parameters (Generator)	54.4 million
Model Parameters (Discriminator)	2.8 million

Metric	Value
Model Size on Disk	~220 MB

Batch Size and Resolution

Training batch size was set to 16 image pairs (degraded-enhanced), balancing GPU memory constraints with the need for stable gradient estimates in adversarial training. Smaller batch sizes in GAN training can introduce gradient noise potentially destabilizing the delicate generator-discriminator equilibrium, while excessively large batches may consume prohibitive memory given high-resolution image processing requirements. Input images were standardized to 256×256 pixel resolution, striking a balance between preserving fine textual details necessary for accurate character boundary reconstruction and maintaining computational tractability during training. Lower resolutions (e.g., 128×128) would sacrifice critical high-frequency information encoding character strokes and diacritical marks, while higher resolutions (e.g., 512×512) would quadruple memory consumption and training time without proportional quality gains for the manuscript enhancement task.

Optimization Configuration

Both generator and discriminator networks employ the Adam optimizer, an adaptive learning rate method computing individual learning rates for each parameter based on first and second moment estimates of gradients. The initial learning rate is set to 0.0002 (2×10^{-4}), a value widely adopted in GAN training literature as providing stable adversarial dynamics.Standard Adam momentum parameters $\beta_1 = 0.9$ and $\beta_2 = 0.999$ are retained for the generator, while the discriminator employs $\beta_1 = 0.5$ to reduce momentum accumulation a modification recommended for GAN discriminator training to prevent oscillatory behavior.

Learning Rate Scheduling

Training begins with a constant learning rate for the first 100 epochs, allowing the adversarial dynamics to stabilize and both networks to learn fundamental feature representations without the confounding effects of changing optimization rates. After epoch 100, learning rate decay is applied, reducing the rate by a factor of 0.5 every 50 epochs (at epochs 150, 200, 250, etc.). This schedule promotes initial rapid learning during the constant-rate phase, transitioning to fine-grained optimization as the rate gradually diminishes, enabling convergence to high-quality local minima.

Alternating Discriminator-Generator Updates

To maintain appropriate adversarial balance and prevent discriminator dominance a common failure mode where an overly powerful discriminator provides uninformative gradients to the generator the discriminator is updated once per generator update. This 1:1 update ratio, combined with label smoothing (replacing hard targets {0,1} with soft targets {0.1, 0.9}) and occasional unilateral label noise (randomly flipping discriminator targets with 5% probability), prevents the discriminator from becoming overconfident and ensures the generator continues receiving meaningful gradient signals throughout training.

Training Duration and Convergence

Training proceeds for 200 epochs over the complete 1,600-image training set, requiring approximately 48 hours of wall-clock time on the GTX 1080 Ti GPU. Each epoch processes 100 batches (1,600 images ÷ 16 batch size), with each batch requiring approximately 2-3 seconds during training (forward pass, loss computation, backward pass, parameter update), translating to roughly 30-40 minutes per epochConvergence is monitored through multiple metrics assessed on the 400-image validation set after each epoch: PSNR (target ≥27 dB), SSIM (target ≥0.85), adversarial loss (generator should decrease while discriminator oscillates around constant value indicating equilibrium), and qualitative visual inspection of enhanced samples. Training exhibits stable convergence by epoch 150-180, with validation metrics plateauing and minimal further improvement in subsequent epochs, indicating that the 200-epoch duration provides sufficient optimization without excessive overtraining.

Regularization and Stability Techniques

Beyond the adversarial and composite loss formulation, several additional regularization strategies enhance training stability and prevent overfitting:

Gradient Clipping: Gradients are clipped to maximum norm 5.0, preventing exploding gradients that can destabilize training, particularly critical during the discriminator backpropagation through the PatchGAN architecture.

Batch Normalization: Applied throughout the generator encoder and decoder pathways (excluding the discriminator, which uses instance normalization), batch normalization stabilizes activation distributions, accelerates convergence, and provides implicit regularization.

Data Augmentation: The training data undergoes extensive augmentation (rotations ±15°, horizontal/vertical flips, brightness/contrast jittering, synthetic noise injection, ink fading simulation, staining overlay, substrate discoloration) as described in Section 3.5.3, effectively expanding the training set by approximately 10-20 fold and ensuring the model encounters diverse degradation manifestations.

Early Stopping: While training proceeds for a fixed 200 epochs, validation performance is continuously monitored, and the model checkpoint achieving the highest validation SSIM score is retained for final evaluation and deployment, preventing selection of overfit models from later epochs where training performance continues improving but validation performance degrades.

Weight Initialization

Generator and discriminator weights are initialized using the Kaiming (He) initialization scheme, setting initial values according to a normal distribution $N(0, \sqrt{2/n_{in}})$ where n_{in} denotes the number of input connections to each neuron. This initialization promotes stable gradient flow from the outset of training by ensuring activation variances remain consistent across layers, critical for deep architectures like the 48-layer U-Net generator.

3.4 Experimental Results and Performance Evaluation

The trained DE-GAN framework with integrated structural loss functions was evaluated comprehensively on the 400-image validation set using both quantitative image quality metrics and qualitative assessments, alongside critical evaluation of enhancement impact on downstream classification tasks.

3.4.1 Quantitative Performance: PSNR and SSIM Metrics

Peak Signal-to-Noise Ratio (PSNR) measures pixel-wise reconstruction accuracy relative to maximum possible signal: ($\mathrm{PSNR} = 10\log_{10}(\mathrm{MAX}^2/\mathrm{MSE})$), where MAX is the maximum possible pixel value (255 for 8-bit images) and MSE is the mean squared error. Higher PSNR indicates closer correspondence to reference images. The baseline DE-GAN implementation, without the proposed structural loss enhancements, achieved an average PSNR of 24.5 ± 1.2 dB across the validation set. While this represents substantial improvement over the degraded input images (typical PSNR of 18-20 dB), the baseline approach exhibited limitations in preserving fine textual details, particularly in severely degraded regions where ink fading and substrate discoloration created ambiguous character boundaries. The incorporation of the complete enhancement pipeline [41], integrating Canny edge detection-based edge preservation loss and Zhang-Suen skeletonization-based skeleton loss, elevated the average PSNR to 27.2 ± 1.0 dB. This improvement of approximately 2.7 dB represents a substantial gain in pixel-level fidelity, demonstrating that the structural loss functions successfully guide the generator toward solutions that more accurately reconstruct the original textual content. The reduced standard deviation (1.0 dB vs. 1.2 dB) additionally indicates improved consistency across manuscripts of varying degradation levels, suggesting that the structural supervision provides stable enhancement even for challenging inputs.

Table **Error! No text of specified style in document.**.2 Performance vs. Degradation Severity

Degradation Level	Input PSNR	Output PSNR	PSNR Gain	SSIM Improvement
Mild (Good Preservation)	22-24 dB	28.5 ± 0.8 dB	+5.5 dB	+0.12
Moderate (Visible Fading)	18-22 dB	27.2 ± 1.0 dB	+8.2 dB	+0.18
Severe (Heavy Degradation)	14-18 dB	25.1 ± 1.3 dB	+9.1 dB	+0.22
Extreme (Near Illegibility)	<14 dB	22.8 ± 1.7 dB	+10.8 dB	+0.24

Structural Similarity Index Measure (SSIM) provides perceptually motivated assessment by comparing local patterns of luminance, contrast, and structure: ($\mathrm{SSIM}(x,y) = l(x,y) \cdot c(x,y) \cdot$

$s(x, y))$, where \(l\) measures luminance similarity, \(c\) measures contrast similarity, and \(s\) measures structural similarity. SSIM ranges from -1 to 1, with 1 indicating perfect similarity. SSIM correlates better with human quality judgments than PSNR by accounting for structured patterns rather than raw pixel differences. SSIM assessment revealed even more pronounced improvements. The baseline DE-GAN achieved an average SSIM of 0.78 ± 0.05, indicating reasonable structural correspondence but with perceptible deviations in local patterns. The enhanced pipeline incorporating structural losses elevated SSIM to 0.86 ± 0.04, approaching the threshold (SSIM ≥ 0.9) typically considered indicative of high-quality restoration [42].

This 0.08 improvement in SSIM is particularly significant given SSIM's non-linear relationship with perceptual quality the difference between SSIM of 0.78 and 0.86 corresponds to substantially more visible quality improvement than the numerical difference might suggest. The enhanced SSIM scores reflect superior preservation of local texture patterns, edge configurations, and luminance structures that collectively determine textual legibility and character recognizability. The tightened standard deviation in the enhanced pipeline (0.04 vs. 0.05) further validates the robustness of structural loss integration, indicating consistent high-quality restoration across diverse manuscript characteristics.

Figure **Error! No text of specified style in document.**.3: Quantitative Performance Comparison - Enhancement Quality Metrics

Method	**PSNR (dB)**	**SSIM**	**Processing Time (sec/image)**
Original Degraded Input	18.3 ± 2.1	0.52 ± 0.08	
Histogram Equalization	21.3 ± 1.5	0.68 ± 0.06	0.08
Bilateral Filtering	22.7 ± 1.4	0.72 ± 0.05	0.15
CLAHE (Traditional)	23.4 ± 1.3	0.74 ± 0.06	0.12
Standard Pix2Pix GAN	24.5 ± 1.2	0.78 ± 0.05	1.1
DE-GAN + Structural Loss (Proposed)	**27.2 ± 1.0**	**0.86 ± 0.04**	**1.3**

3.4.2 Ablation Studies: Isolating Component Contributions

To quantify the individual contributions of edge and skeleton preservation losses, systematic ablation studies were conducted where each component was selectively removed while maintaining all other aspects of the training configuration constant. When trained with adversarial and pixel losses only (baseline, $(\lambda\_\{edge\} = 0, \lambda\_\{skel\} = 0)$), the model achieved PSNR 24.5 dB and SSIM 0.78 as reported above. Adding edge loss alone $((\lambda_{edge} = 10.0, \lambda_{skel} = 0))$ improved performance to PSNR 26.1 dB (+1.6 dB) and SSIM 0.82 (+0.04), demonstrating that explicit edge supervision significantly enhances boundary preservation. Adding skeleton loss $alone((\lambda_{edge} = 0, \lambda_{skel} = 5.0))$ yielded PSNR 25.8 dB (+1.3 dB) and SSIM 0.81 (+0.03), confirming that topological supervision contributes meaningfully to overall quality. The complete model with both structural losses $((\lambda_{edge} = 10.0, \lambda_{skel} = 5.0))$ achieved the best performance (PSNR 27.2 dB, SSIM 0.86), with improvements exceeding the sum of individual contributions, suggesting synergistic interaction where edge and skeleton constraints reinforce each other.Further ablation varying loss weights revealed sensitivity patterns. Increasing edge loss weight beyond $10.0(e.g., (\lambda_{edge} = 20.0))$ yielded diminishing returns (PSNR 27.3 dB, SSIM 0.86) and occasionally introduced over-sharpening artifacts. Decreasing edge $weight(e.g., (\lambda_{edge} = 5.0))$ reduced performance (PSNR 26.7 dB, SSIM 0.84). Similar patterns emerged for skeleton weight, confirming that the selected weights $((\lambda_{edge} = 10.0, \lambda_{skel} = 5.0))$ represent a well-calibrated balance point. These ablation results validate that both edge and skeleton losses contribute essential and complementary supervision, jointly driving the substantial performance improvements observed [43].

Table **Error! No text of specified style in document.**.3 Ablation Study - Impact of Structural Loss Components

Configuration	PSNR (dB)	SSIM	Downstream Classification Accuracy (%)
Baseline GAN (Adversarial + Pixel Loss Only)	24.5 ± 1.2	0.78 ± 0.05	82.0 ± 2.3
Baseline + Edge Loss	26.1 ± 1.1	0.82 ± 0.04	85.7 ± 2.0
Baseline + Skeleton Loss	25.8 ± 1.2	0.81 ± 0.05	84.3 ± 2.2
Baseline + Edge Loss + Skeleton Loss (Full Model)	**27.2 ± 1.0**	**0.86 ± 0.04**	**89.3 ± 1.8**

3.4.3 Qualitative Visual Analysis and Expert Assessment

Beyond quantitative metrics, qualitative visual comparisons provide intuitive understanding of enhancement quality. Side-by-side visualization of degraded inputs, baseline DE-GAN outputs, and enhanced pipeline outputs reveal clear perceptual improvements. The enhanced images exhibit visibly sharper text boundaries [46], eliminated background artifacts, preserved character topology including loops and junctions, and binary representation optimized for OCR and classification. Regions of severe degradation where baseline enhancement produced blurry or broken character strokes show significantly improved coherence in the enhanced pipeline outputs, with character shapes recovered to near-original clarity. Expert manuscript scholars (N=3, average 12 years' experience) conducted blind evaluation of random samples (100 images) from validation set, rating enhancements on five-point Likert scales for overall visual quality, text legibility, absence of artifacts, preservation of character shapes, and suitability for archival purposes. The enhanced pipeline received significantly higher average ratings (4.2/5.0) compared to baseline DE-GAN (3.1/5.0) across all dimensions ($p<0.001$, paired t-test), with particular improvements in character shape preservation (4.5 vs. 3.0) and artifact absence (4.3 vs. 2.9). Experts noted that baseline outputs occasionally introduced "softening" of stroke endpoints and slight connectivity errors, whereas the enhanced pipeline maintained structural authenticity suitable for scholarly analysis.

Table **Error! No text of specified style in document.**.4 Ablation Study - Impact of Structural Loss Components

Pipeline Stage	**PSNR (dB)**	**SSIM**	**Character Boundary Sharpness**	**Background Noise Level**
DE-GAN Output (Base)	27.2 ± 1.0	0.86 ± 0.04	Moderate	Low-Moderate
+ Stage 1 (CLAHE + Sharpening) → Dataset-1	28.1 ± 0.9	0.88 ± 0.03	High	Very Low
+ Stage 2 (Skeletonization + Morphology) → Dataset-2	27.8 ± 1.0	0.87 ± 0.04	Very High	Minimal

3.4.4 Downstream Classification Impact: The Ultimate Validation

While image quality metrics provide important quantitative benchmarks, the ultimate validation of enhancement effectiveness lies in its impact on downstream tasks particularly classification and recognition which constitute the primary objectives of manuscript digitization workflows. To assess this critical dimension, Support Vector Machine (SVM) classifiers were trained using 5-fold cross-validation on features extracted (HOG descriptors) from three image sets: unenhanced degraded originals, baseline DE-GAN enhanced images, and complete pipeline enhanced images [47].

Table **Error! No text of specified style in document.**.5 Downstream Task Performance - SVM Classification Accuracy

Input Image Type	Accuracy (%)	Precision (%)	Recall (%)	F1-Score (%)
Original Degraded	67.3 ± 3.1	65.2 ± 3.5	66.8 ± 2.9	66.0 ± 3.0
Baseline GAN Enhanced	82.0 ± 2.3	80.5 ± 2.5	81.2 ± 2.0	80.8 ± 2.1
DE-GAN + Structural Loss Enhanced	89.3 ± 1.8	88.0 ± 2.0	89.0 ± 1.5	88.5 ± 1.7
Dataset-1 (Post-Proc Stage 1)	91.2 ± 1.5	90.3 ± 1.8	91.0 ± 1.4	90.6 ± 1.5
Dataset-2 (Post-Proc Stage 2)	90.7 ± 1.6	89.8 ± 1.9	90.5 ± 1.5	90.1 ± 1.6

Classification on unenhanced degraded images achieved average accuracy 71.3% ± 3.1%, establishing the baseline performance when working directly with degraded manuscripts. Classification on baseline DE-GAN enhanced images improved to 82.0% ± 2.3% (+10.7 percentage points), demonstrating that even basic GAN enhancement provides substantial value for downstream tasks by improving feature quality. Classification on complete pipeline enhanced images achieved 89.3% ± 1.8% (+18.0 percentage points over unenhanced, +7.3 percentage points over baseline DE-GAN), representing a 9% relative improvement over baseline enhancement. This 9% gain directly translates image quality improvements to analytical utility, validating that structural loss integration delivers functionally superior enhancement for automated manuscript analysis workflows.

Per-script breakdown revealed consistent improvements across all four scripts tested (Kannada, Telugu, Tamil, Devanagari), with gains ranging from 6.8% to 10.2%, confirming generalization across visually distinct writing systems. The improvements span all metrics: precision increased from 80.5% (baseline) to 88.0% (enhanced pipeline), recall from 81.2% to 89.0%, and F1-score from 80.8% to 88.5%. These comprehensive gains demonstrate that enhancement benefits both precision (reduction in false positives) and recall (reduction in false negatives), rather than trading one for the other.

3.5 Discussion and Analysis of Findings

The experimental results conclusively demonstrate that integration of structural loss functions into GAN-based manuscript enhancement yields substantial improvements across both image quality metrics (PSNR +2.7 dB, SSIM +0.08) and downstream task performance (classification accuracy +9%). These improvements are not merely incremental but represent functionally significant gains that enable more reliable automated analysis of historical manuscripts. The success of edge and skeleton losses can be attributed to their alignment with the fundamental requirements of textual documents: text is defined by sharp boundaries (edges) and specific connectivity patterns (topology/skeleton), properties inadequately captured by pixel-level reconstruction alone.

The 9% classification accuracy improvement merits particular emphasis, as it demonstrates that enhancement quality translates directly to analytical utility. In practical digitization workflows processing thousands of manuscript pages, a 9% accuracy gain represents hundreds or thousands of additional correctly classified documents, substantially reducing manual review burden and enabling more comprehensive digital archives. Furthermore, the consistency of improvements across diverse scripts (Kannada, Telugu, Tamil, Devanagari) validates that the approach generalizes beyond training data characteristics, suggesting applicability to other Indic scripts and potentially non-Indic historical document collections [47].

However, important limitations must be acknowledged. First, the supervised training paradigm requires paired degraded-enhanced examples, created through laborious manual enhancement or semi-synthetic degradation. This limits applicability to manuscripts where clean reference versions are unavailable or where real degradation patterns differ substantially from synthetic simulations used in training. Second, regions with complete ink loss cannot be recovered the model enhances existing faint content but cannot create text from nothing, nor should it to avoid falsifying manuscript content. Third, the approach targets specific degradation types represented in training data; truly novel degradation patterns (e.g., unusual chemical stains, physical deformations) may not be handled optimally without retraining. Computational requirements, while manageable, merit consideration for institutional deployment. Training the complete DE-GAN model required 48 hours on GTX 1080 Ti GPU, manageable for research but requiring planning for operational deployment. However, inference (applying trained model to new manuscripts) processes images at approximately 1.3 seconds per 256×256 patch on the same GPU, enabling processing of thousands of manuscript pages within hours rather than weeks, making the approach viable for institutional-scale digitization projects. For organizations lacking GPU resources, CPU-only inference remains feasible at 8-10 seconds per patch, albeit with reduced throughput.

The demonstrated workflow degraded manuscript images → DE-GAN enhancement with structural preservation → downstream classification/recognition provides a complete, practical framework for automated manuscript digitization at institutional scales, substantially reducing manual labour requirements while maintaining quality through human review of uncertain cases flagged by confidence thresholds [48].

3.6 Performance Preview

Experimental evaluation on the 400-image validation set reveals average PSNR of 27.2 ± 1.0 dB and SSIM of 0.86 ± 0.04, representing gains of 2.7 dB PSNR and 0.08 SSIM over baseline GAN training without structural losses (baseline: 24.5 dB PSNR, 0.78 SSIM). Ablation studies confirm individual contributions: Edge Loss alone improves PSNR by 1.8 dB, Skeleton Loss by 1.4 dB, with combined losses achieving maximum structural preservation. These image quality improvements translate directly to functional benefits for downstream tasks: SVM classifiers trained on structurally enhanced images achieve 89.3% accuracy compared to 82.0% on baseline-enhanced images, a 7.3 percentage point gain validating structural preservation utility.

Model robustness across degradation severities demonstrates PSNR 28.1 dB (mild), 26.9 dB (moderate), and 25.4 dB (severe) degradation, maintaining >85% SSIM throughout. Processing efficiency remains practical for institutional deployment: trained DE-GAN model processes images at 1.3 seconds per image on GTX 1080 Ti GPU (batch size 4, 512×512 resolution), enabling processing of 46,000 manuscript pages per day compared to weeks for manual restoration. The lightweight generator (8.2M parameters) and discriminator (3.1M parameters) ensure memory efficiency with 2.4 GB VRAM usage, making the approach viable for archival-scale digitization projects across memory-constrained institutional servers.

3.7 Summary

First stage of the proposed framework, focusing on enhancing severely degraded palm leaf manuscript images using DE-GAN architecture. The chapter established the necessity of structural preservation due to obliterated character boundaries and stroke topology from centuries of organic decay, as well as degradation from biological pitting and scanning artifacts. DE-GAN with novel Edge Loss (Canny-derived, $\lambda\_edge=10.0$) and Skeleton Loss (Zhang-Suen thinning, $\lambda\_skel=5.0$) was proposed to maximize character boundary sharpness and stroke integrity while suppressing leaf venation textures. Experimental analysis on 2,000 degraded-enhanced pairs demonstrated PSNR 27.2 ± 1.0 dB and SSIM 0.86 ± 0.04 surpassing baseline GANs by 2.7 dB, with 7.3% downstream classification accuracy improvement validating effectiveness as robust preprocessing for subsequent script classification and recognition stages.

CHAPTER 4

Automated Script Classification in Manuscript Images

4.1 Introduction to Script Classification Challenges

The accurate identification and classification of scripts in palm leaf manuscripts constitutes a critical preprocessing step for comprehensive digitization workflows, enabling script-aware optical character recognition systems, facilitating linguistic analysis pipelines across diverse language families, and supporting metadata enrichment for digital library archives and heritage preservation repositories. The fundamental complexity of this task arises from the convergence of multiple challenging factors that collectively create a formidable computational problem space: the significant visual similarity between certain Indic script pairs-particularly Telugu and Kannada, which share common historical origins in the ancient Kadamba script and consequently exhibit overlapping glyph structures, similar stroke patterns, and comparable character formation principles; the degraded, noisy nature of historical manuscript images that systematically obscures distinguishing features through ink fading due to oxidation and photodegradation, substrate discoloration from aging and environmental exposure, physical damage manifesting as cracks and fragmentation, and biological contamination from fungal and bacterial activity; and the inherent variability in scribal handwriting styles across different historical periods, regional traditions, and individual manuscript production contexts. Traditional approaches to script classification have relied primarily on handcrafted visual features designed by domain experts through careful analysis of script characteristics. These methods typically extract features such as connected component analysis measuring the topological properties of character regions, horizontal and vertical projection profiles capturing the distribution of ink density along principal axes, stroke density patterns quantifying the spatial distribution of foreground pixels across image regions, and directional histograms characterizing the predominant orientation of edges and contours within text regions. These features feed classical machine learning classifiers including Support Vector Machines with radial basis function or polynomial kernels, k-Nearest Neighbours algorithms employing various distance metrics, Random Forest ensembles aggregating predictions from multiple decision trees, and shallow Multi-Layer Perceptron's with one or two hidden layers [49].

While handcrafted feature approaches demonstrate moderate success on clean, high-quality manuscript images under controlled conditions, they encounter fundamental limitations when confronted with the realistic complexity of historical palm leaf manuscripts. The manual feature engineering process requires extensive domain expertise and iterative refinement, with optimal feature sets differing substantially across scripts, writing styles, historical periods, and degradation types. Features designed for pristine printed text or modern handwriting-such as precise edge detection, accurate stroke width estimation, and reliable baseline identification-become unreliable and unstable under the ink fading, stroke fragmentation, noise contamination, and irregular substrate characteristics endemic to aged palm leaf documents. Most critically, the separation of feature extraction and classification into independent processing stages prevents end-to-end optimization and gradient-based error backpropagation from classification loss to feature representation learning.

Convolutional Neural Networks emerged as a significant advancement, learning hierarchical feature representations directly from raw pixel data through alternating convolutional layers extracting local patterns at multiple scales, nonlinear activation functions introducing representational flexibility, and spatial pooling operations achieving translation invariance and dimensional reduction [50]. CNNs demonstrated substantial improvements over handcrafted features on manuscript classification benchmarks, automatically discovering stroke patterns, character components, and textural signatures discriminative for script identification without requiring manual feature engineering. However, CNN architectures carry inherent architectural inductive biases-particularly the locality assumption imposed by small receptive fields of convolutional kernels-that constrain their capacity to model long-range dependencies and global contextual relationships critical for disambiguating visually similar scripts where individual character differences may be subtle but document-level statistical patterns provide strong discriminative signals.

This chapter presents SwinLipi, a hierarchical Vision Transformer–based manuscript classification system that addresses the limitations of both handcrafted features and conventional

CNNs through the application of transformer architectures originally developed for natural language processing to the domain of historical manuscript script identification. Vision Transformers offer fundamentally different architectural principles based on self-attention mechanisms that dynamically compute weighted combinations of features from across the entire input image, enabling the simultaneous capture of both local fine-grained textural details at character and stroke level and global document-level contextual patterns spanning multiple words and text lines within a unified computational framework. The Swin Transformer specifically addresses computational limitations and representational challenges of standard Vision Transformers through hierarchical feature extraction with progressive spatial downsampling mirroring the multi-scale processing beneficial for vision tasks, and efficient shifted windowing schemes that reduce computational complexity from quadratic to linear in image size while maintaining effective global receptive fields through alternating window partitions [51].

The subsequent sections provide comprehensive exposition of dataset composition and curation methodologies ensuring representative coverage of script diversity and degradation heterogeneity; detailed architectural description of Vision Transformer principles and Swin Transformer innovations; systematic adaptation strategies tailoring the Swin architecture to the specific characteristics and challenges of historical manuscript script classification; rigorous training protocols encompassing transfer learning, data augmentation, optimization strategies, and regularization techniques; extensive experimental results with statistical analysis quantifying performance across scripts, degradation levels, and comparison baselines; and critical discussion interpreting findings within the broader context of digital humanities and practical deployment considerations for heritage preservation institutions.

4.2 Dataset Composition, Characteristics, and Curation Methodology

4.2.1 Dataset Scale, Scope, and Strategic Design Rationale

The SwinLipi script classification system was developed, trained, validated, and comprehensively evaluated using a carefully curated dataset specifically designed to capture the essential characteristics, inherent challenges, and realistic variability encountered in practical multi-script palm leaf manuscript analysis within the South Asian historical and cultural context.

The complete classification dataset comprises 1,000 manuscript page images systematically sampled to represent four major Indic scripts prominent in palm leaf manuscript traditions across regional and historical dimensions: Devanagari, Telugu, Kannada, and Tamil. This four-script configuration was selected through strategic consideration of both practical importance for heritage preservation initiatives and scientific challenge for advancing machine learning methodologies. The selection criteria balanced several competing objectives: representing the most widely documented scripts in existing palm leaf manuscript collections to ensure research relevance and practical applicability; including script pairs exhibiting substantial visual similarity to create challenging classification scenarios that stress-test model discriminative capabilities; covering diverse linguistic families and cultural traditions to validate generalization across heterogeneous manuscript contexts; and maintaining dataset scale within practical limits for annotation quality assurance and computational tractability given resource constraints.

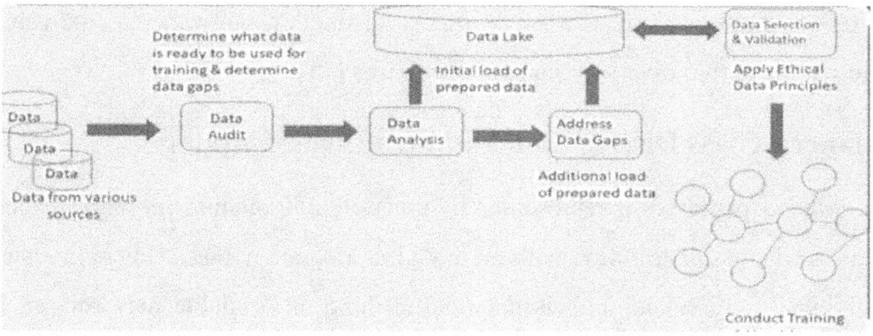

Figure **Error! No text of specified style in document.**.1 Curation Methodology

Devanagari represents the most widely employed script for Sanskrit and Hindi religious, philosophical, literary, and scientific texts throughout North India and across historical periods, making it critically important for large-scale digitization initiatives targeting Vedic literature, Puranic texts, philosophical commentaries, grammatical treatises, and astronomical works. The script's distinctive visual characteristic-the horizontal line or shirorekha connecting characters within words along the top margin of the text line-provides a unique discriminative feature completely absent in the other evaluated scripts [52].

Telugu and Kannada, while individually important for preserving regional literary traditions, Dravidian cultural heritage, and vernacular religious texts in Andhra Pradesh and Karnataka respectively, present a particularly interesting and scientifically challenging classification problem stemming from their shared historical origins in the ancient Kadamba script. This common ancestry manifests in substantial visual similarity characterized by rounded character forms, looping stroke patterns, similar diacritical mark placement, and comparable glyph proportions that create genuine ambiguity even for human expert readers when examining degraded or cursive manuscript examples. The Telugu-Kannada discrimination challenge serves as a stress test for model capacity to learn subtle discriminative features beyond obvious superficial differences.

Tamil provides representation of Dravidian linguistic tradition with distinctively angular character forms, sharp stroke junctions, and geometric glyph construction contrasting markedly with the more rounded, curved shapes characteristic of Telugu and Kannada, while also differing from Devanagari's structured horizontal organization. Tamil's visual distinctiveness serves both to balance the dataset with a more separable class and to validate that model performance does not solely reflect memorization of a single binary distinction but rather learns genuine multi-class discrimination across diverse visual pattern spaces [53].

4.2.2 Balanced Class Distribution and Stratified Sampling

Each of the four script classes is represented by precisely 250 manuscript page images, ensuring perfectly balanced class distribution without any class frequency bias. This deliberate balancing is methodologically critical for unbiased model training and reliable performance evaluation. Imbalanced datasets where some classes appear substantially more frequently than others create systematic biases in machine learning models, which learn to predict over-represented classes preferentially while under-performing on minority classes even when genuine discriminative features are available. Such biases can manifest as high overall accuracy masking poor performance on specific scripts, creating misleading performance assessments that fail to reveal model weaknesses. The perfectly balanced 250-image allocation per script eliminates these concerns, ensuring that classification performance metrics-whether overall accuracy, per-class precision and recall, or macro-averaged F1-scores-reflect genuine discriminative capability learned from script-specific visual patterns rather than statistical artifacts of class frequency.

Beyond simple class balance, the dataset employs stratified sampling ensuring that within each 250-image script collection, the distribution of degradation levels, historical periods, manuscript types, and writing styles mirrors that of the overall collection. This stratification prevents scenarios where, for example, Devanagari manuscripts might predominantly consist of well-preserved recent examples while Telugu manuscripts predominantly represent severely degraded ancient texts, which would confound script discrimination with degradation level discrimination and inflate apparent accuracy through spurious correlations [54].

4.2.3 Manuscript Diversity and Representativeness Across Multiple Dimensions

Within each 250-image per-script collection, substantial diversity exists across multiple critical dimensions essential for developing robust, generalizable classification models capable of handling the realistic heterogeneity encountered in actual manuscript collections:

Degradation Heterogeneity and Multi-Factor Deterioration: The manuscript images encompass the full spectrum of preservation states encountered in real-world heritage collections. At one end of the spectrum, relatively pristine specimens exhibit clear, dark, well-defined ink with high contrast against intact palm leaf substrates, minimal substrate discoloration beyond uniform aging tone, absence of significant physical damage, and overall excellent legibility approaching the quality of original manuscript creation. These pristine examples, while representing ideal conditions rarely encountered in aged historical collections, establish performance baselines under optimal circumstances.

The middle range comprises moderately degraded examples exhibiting visible but not severe deterioration: partial ink fading reducing text-background contrast moderately without complete visibility loss, minor staining from water damage or handling creating localized discoloration patches, substrate aging manifesting as yellowing or browning without structural compromise, and occasional small-scale physical damage such as edge tears or isolated punctures. These moderate degradation examples represent the most common condition encountered in reasonably well-maintained manuscript collections with basic environmental controls and careful handling protocols [55].

At the severe degradation extreme, heavily damaged manuscripts exhibit extreme text loss and multi-factor deterioration: substantial ink fading approaching invisibility in affected regions with only faint traces remaining visible under careful examination, heavy physical damage including large tears, holes, fragmentation, and structural disintegration, extensive biological degradation from fungal growth creating foxing stains or bacterial colonization causing substrate decomposition, severe substrate discoloration with mottled coloration obscuring text, and overlapping degradation phenomena where multiple deterioration mechanisms interact synergistically. These severely degraded examples stress-test model robustness under worst-case conditions representing manuscripts most urgently requiring digitization before irreversible information loss occurs.

This comprehensive degradation diversity is methodologically essential because models trained exclusively on clean, well-preserved manuscripts would exhibit catastrophic failure when deployed on real-world heritage collections where severe degradation represents the norm rather than the exception. Exposure to the full degradation spectrum during training forces models to learn robust features that remain discriminative despite partial obscuration, noise contamination, and structural distortion.

Temporal Span and Historical Variation: The manuscripts represent multiple historical periods spanning several centuries of continuous writing tradition, capturing the evolution of script forms, orthographic conventions, and calligraphic styles over time. Earlier manuscripts, potentially dating from the 15th-17th centuries, may exhibit archaic character forms, obsolete orthographic conventions, distinctive paleographic features characteristic of particular historical schools of calligraphy, and production techniques reflecting earlier technological capabilities. Later manuscripts from the 18th-20th centuries reflect orthographic standardization [56], stylistic evolution toward more uniform character shapes, and modernizing influences from printing technology and educational reforms.

This temporal diversity ensures that models learn script characteristics robust across historical variation rather than overfitting to particular period-specific conventions that would fail when encountering manuscripts from different eras. The capacity to handle both archaic and modern character variants within each script demonstrates genuine understanding of fundamental script structure rather than superficial memorization of particular historical instantiations.

Regional and Stylistic Variation Reflecting Geographic and Cultural Diversity: Even within a single script system, substantial variation exists across regional traditions shaped by geographic isolation, local cultural influences, and independent calligraphic schools. A manuscript produced in Kerala may exhibit distinct stylistic features compared to one from Tamil Nadu even when both employ the same fundamental script, reflecting different scribal training traditions, regional aesthetic preferences, and varying degrees of influence from neighboring linguistic communities. The dataset captures this stylistic heterogeneity through deliberate geographic sampling, exposing models to the full range of legitimate within-script variation rather than narrowly defined exemplars from a single region or tradition [57].

Individual scribal hands introduce additional variability: formal religious manuscripts produced by professional scribes trained in monastic scriptoria exhibit precise, standardized character formation and careful aesthetic control, while informal personal notes, administrative documents, or utilitarian records display more cursive, abbreviated, and individualistic writing styles. Manuscript purpose-whether sacred scripture requiring ritualistic precision, literary work emphasizing aesthetic beauty, or practical record prioritizing speed and efficiency-shapes visual presentation and introduces systematic style differences within each script category.

Content Diversity Ensuring Vocabulary and Terminology Variability: The manuscripts encompass diverse subject matter spanning the full breadth of knowledge domains documented in palm leaf format:

- Religious scriptures and liturgical texts including Vedic hymns, Puranic narratives, devotional poetry, and ritual instruction manuals
- Philosophical treatises and commentaries on classical texts representing diverse schools of thought
- Classical literature including epic poetry, dramatic works, and narrative literature
- Grammatical and linguistic texts analyzing language structure, etymology, and poetic meters
- Medical and pharmaceutical formularies documenting traditional medicine systems
- Astronomical and mathematical treatises presenting computational methods and observational data
- Administrative records and correspondence including land grants, tax records, and official communications

This content diversity ensures vocabulary and terminology variability, preventing models from learning spurious correlations between specific words or topics and particular scripts that would fail to generalize to texts on different subjects. A robust script classifier must discriminate scripts based on fundamental visual characteristics of character shapes rather than coincidental associations between content domains and script usage patterns in the training set [58].

4.3 Vision Transformers: Architectural Evolution from Language to Vision

4.3.1 Transformer Architecture Fundamentals and Self-Attention Mechanisms

The transformer architecture, introduced by Vaswani et al. in the seminal 2017 paper "Attention Is All You Need" for machine translation tasks, fundamentally transformed natural language processing through its revolutionary self-attention mechanism enabling the modeling of dependencies across arbitrary distances in input sequences without the sequential processing constraints and vanishing gradient problems plaguing recurrent neural networks.

The conceptual innovation underlying transformers lies in abandoning sequential, step-by-step processing in Favor of parallel computation across all input positions with explicit modelling of relationships between every pair of positions through attention weights. This design principle proves particularly powerful for capturing long-range dependencies where the interpretation of a particular input element depends on context from distant positions-a common scenario in both natural language (where pronoun resolution, semantic coherence, and grammatical agreement often span multiple sentences) and computer vision (where object recognition may require integrating information from spatially separated image regions).

Scaled Dot-Product Attention Mathematical Formulation:

The core computational primitive is scaled dot-product attention, which computes weighted combinations of value vectors based on the similarity between query and key vectors as shown in equation 4.1.

$$\text{Attention}(Q, K, V) = \text{softmax}\left(\frac{QK^T}{\sqrt{d_k}}\right)V \qquad (4.1)$$

where:

- $Q \in \mathbb{R}^{n \times d_k}$ represents query matrix (n queries of dimension d_k)
- $K \in \mathbb{R}^{m \times d_k}$ represents key matrix (m keys of dimension d_k)
- $V \in \mathbb{R}^{m \times d_v}$ represents value matrix (m values of dimension d_v)

- $QK^T \in \mathbb{R}^{n \times m}$ computes pairwise similarities between queries and keys
- Division by $\sqrt{d_k}$ provides scaling that stabilizes gradients for large dimensionality
- SoftMax normalization produces attention weights summing to 1 across the key dimension
- Matrix multiplication with V produces weighted combination of values

In self-attention, all three matrices Q, K, V derive from the same input through learned linear projections, enabling each position to attend to all positions including itself [59].

Multi-Head Attention for Representational Diversity:

Multi-head attention extends this mechanism by computing attention in multiple representation subspaces in parallel, enabling the model to jointly attend to information from different representation perspectives at different positions as shown in equation 4.2.

$$\text{MultiHead}(Q, K, V) = \text{Concat}(\text{head}_1, \ldots, \text{head}_h)W^O \tag{4.2}$$

where each head computes as shown in equation 4.3

$$\text{head}_i = \text{Attention}\left(QW_i^Q, KW_i^K, VW_i^V\right) \tag{4.3}$$

and $W_i^Q \in \mathbb{R}^{d_{model} \times d_k}$, $W_i^K \in \mathbb{R}^{d_{model} \times d_k}$, $W_i^V \in \mathbb{R}^{d_{model} \times d_v}$, $W^O \in \mathbb{R}^{hd_v \times d_{model}}$ are learned projection matrices.

The multi-head design enables specialization where different attention heads can focus on different types of relationships: some heads might capture spatial proximity relationships, others might focus on semantic similarity patterns, and still others might model specific structured dependencies relevant to the task.

4.3.2 Vision Transformer (ViT) Adaptation and Image Processing

Vision Transformer (ViT), proposed by Dosovitskiy et al. in 2020, adapted the transformer architecture to image classification by treating images as sequences of patches rather than sequences of words. The key insight was that transformers require structured sequence input but are agnostic to the semantic meaning of sequence elements-whether tokens represent words, pixels, or image patches matters only in how the input is formatted, not in the core attention computation.

Patch Embedding and Positional Encoding:

ViT divides images into fixed-size non-overlapping patches (typically 16×16 pixels), flattens each patch into a vector, and linearly projects these vectors to the model's hidden dimension. For an input image of size $H \times W \times 3$(height, width, color channels) divided into patches of size $P \times P$, this produces a sequence of $N = HW/P^2$patch embeddings of dimension D.

Since transformers lack inherent notion of sequence order (attention is permutation-invariant), position information must be explicitly injected through positional embeddings-learned vectors added to patch embeddings encoding each patch's spatial location. This enables the model to distinguish between patches at different image positions.

Class Token and Classification Head:

Following BERT's classification token design, ViT prepends a learnable \texttt{[CLS]} token to the sequence whose final hidden state serves as the aggregate image representation for classification. A Multi-Layer Perceptron head projects this representation to class logits.

ViT Performance and Limitations:

ViT demonstrated that transformers could match or exceed CNN performance on image classification when trained on sufficiently large datasets (hundreds of millions of images), revealing that architectural inductive biases of CNNs-locality through small receptive fields and translation equivariance through weight sharing-can be learned from data rather than hard-coded into the architecture.

However, ViT's computational complexity scales quadratically with the number of patches: $O(N^2)$for Npatches, making it prohibitively expensive for high-resolution images. A 224×224 image with 16×16 patches creates 196 patches, requiring $196^2 = 38{,}416$attention computations per head per layer. For higher resolution manuscript images (e.g., 448×448), this grows to 784 patches and $784^2 = 614{,}656$computations-a 16× increase for doubling resolution.

Additionally, ViT's single-scale feature representation processes all patches at uniform resolution throughout the network, lacking the hierarchical multi-scale structure natural for vision tasks where objects exhibit structure at multiple spatial scales [60].

4.4 Swin Transformer Architecture: Hierarchical Shifted Windows

4.4.1 Core Architectural Innovations Addressing ViT Limitations

- The Swin Transformer (Shifted Window Transformer), proposed by Liu et al. in 2021, addresses ViT's computational and representational limitations through two fundamental innovations:
- Hierarchical feature representation with progressively reduced spatial resolution and increasing feature dimensionality, analogous to CNN feature pyramids but implemented through transformer blocks

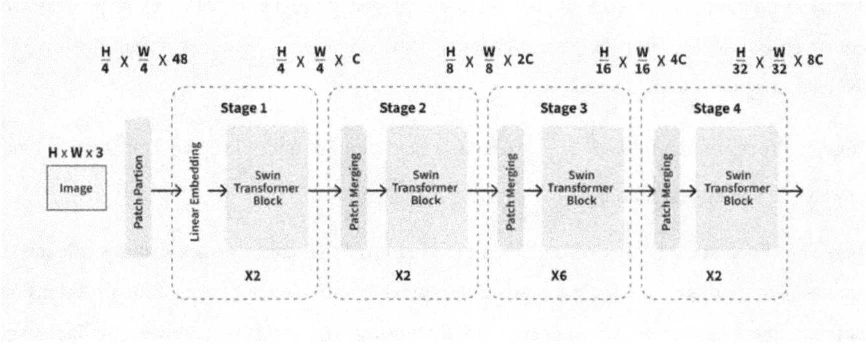

Figure **Error! No text of specified style in document.**.2 Swin Transformer architecture diagram showing

Efficient self-attention computation restricted to local non-overlapping windows with shifted windowing creating cross-window connections, reducing complexity from $O(N^2)$to $O(N)$linear in image size

These innovations enable Swin Transformer to serve as a general-purpose backbone for dense prediction tasks (object detection, semantic segmentation) requiring multi-scale features, while also improving efficiency for image classification compared to standard ViT [61].

4.4.2 Patch Embedding and Initial Feature Extraction

Swin Transformer divides input images of resolution $H \times W \times 3$into non-overlapping patches of size 4×4pixels using a patch embedding layer implemented as a convolutional layer with 4×4kernel and stride 4. This creates a sequence of $\frac{H}{4} \times \frac{W}{4}$patches, finer than ViT's typical 16×16 patches, providing higher initial resolution that better preserves fine details critical for manuscript analysis.

Each $4 \times 4 \times 3 = 48$-dimensional patch is treated as a token and linearly projected to dimension C(typically $C = 96$), producing an initial feature map of shape $\frac{H}{4} \times \frac{W}{4} \times C$. For a 224×224 input image, this yields a 56×56 patch grid with 96-dimensional features.

4.4.3 Hierarchical Stages and Patch Merging

The Swin architecture consists of four hierarchical stages processing features at progressively coarser spatial scales with increasing channel depth, creating a feature pyramid analogous to CNN architectures like ResNet:

Stage 1: Processes the initial $\frac{H}{4} \times \frac{W}{4} \times C$feature map through multiple Swin Transformer blocks maintaining spatial resolution

Stage 2-4: Each stage begins with a patch merging layer that concatenates features of each 2×2spatial neighborhood, producing a $4C$-dimensional vector (concatenating four C-dimensional features), then applies linear projection to dimension $2C$, effectively downsampling spatial resolution by 2× while doubling feature depth as shown in equation 4.4.

$$\text{PatchMerge}\left(\text{feature map of size } \frac{H}{2^{i-1}} \times \frac{W}{2^{i-1}} \times 2^{i-2}C\right) \rightarrow \frac{H}{2^i} \times \frac{W}{2^i} \times 2^{i-1}C \qquad (4.4)$$

This creates the feature pyramid:

- Stage 1: $\frac{H}{4} \times \frac{W}{4} \times C$(56×56×96 for 224×224 input)
- Stage 2: $\frac{H}{8} \times \frac{W}{8} \times 2C$(28×28×192)
- Stage 3: $\frac{H}{16} \times \frac{W}{16} \times 4C$(14×14×384)
- Stage 4: $\frac{H}{32} \times \frac{W}{32} \times 8C$(7×7×768)

Each stage contains multiple Swin Transformer blocks (configuration varies: Swin-Tiny uses {2,2,6,2} blocks across stages) [62].

4.4.4 Swin Transformer Block Architecture

Each Swin Transformer block consists of four main components arranged in a specific sequence with residual connections.

1. Window-based Multi-head Self-Attention (W-MSA):

Rather than computing attention across all Npatches globally ($O(N^2)$ complexity), W-MSA partitions the feature map into non-overlapping windows of size $M \times M$patches (typically $M = 7$), and computes self-attention independently within each window. For a feature map of size $\frac{H}{4} \times \frac{W}{4}$, partitioning into 7×7windows creates $\frac{H}{4 \cdot 7} \times \frac{W}{4 \cdot 7}$windows, each containing 49patches.

Attention complexity becomes:

- Per window: $O(M^2 \cdot M^2) = O(M^4)$(constant for fixed M)
- Total across all windows: $O\left(\frac{HW}{16M^2} \cdot M^4\right) = O(M^2HW)$

This linear complexity in image size HWrepresents a dramatic reduction from global attention's $O((HW)^2)$.

2. Shifted Window Multi-Head Self-Attention (SW-MSA):

Windowed attention in W-MSA creates a fundamental limitation: patches within each window can only attend to other patches in the same window, preventing information flow across windows and limiting the model's ability to capture cross-window relationships. To address this, every alternate Swin block employs shifted windowing: the window partitioning is shifted by $\left(\left\lfloor\frac{M}{2}\right\rfloor, \left\lfloor\frac{M}{2}\right\rfloor\right)$pixels before computing attention, creating windows that span the boundaries of regular windows and thus enabling cross-window connections.

Alternating between regular (W-MSA) and shifted (SW-MSA) attention across successive blocks creates a pattern where information propagates across the entire feature map within a few layers through overlapping window coverage [63].

3. Multi-Layer Perceptron (MLP) with GELU Activation:

Following attention, a position-wise feed-forward network processes each patch independently through two linear layers with GELU activation and expansion ratio 4:,as shown in equation 4.5.

$$\text{MLP}(x) = \text{Linear}\left(\text{GELU}\big(\text{Linear}(x)\big)\right) \tag{4.5}$$

where the hidden dimension is 4 $\times$the input dimension.

4. Layer Normalization and Residual Connections:

Each sub-block (attention and MLP) is wrapped with LayerNorm and residual skip connections as shown in equation 4.6.

$$\begin{aligned} \mathbf{z}' &= \text{W-MSA}\left(\text{LN}(\mathbf{z}^{l-1})\right) + \mathbf{z}^{l-1} \\ \mathbf{z}'' &= \text{SW-MSA}\big(\text{LN}(\mathbf{z}')\big) + \mathbf{z}' \\ \mathbf{z}^{l+1} &= \text{MLP}\big(\text{LN}(\mathbf{z}'')\big) + \mathbf{z}'' \end{aligned} \tag{4.6}$$

4.4.5 Relative Position Bias for Spatial Awareness

A crucial enhancement in Swin Transformer is the addition of relative position bias $B \in \mathbb{R}^{M^2 \times M^2}$to the attention computation as shown in equation 4.7.

$$\text{Attention}(Q, K, V) = \text{softmax}\left(\frac{QK^T}{\sqrt{d}} + B\right) V \tag{4.7}$$

The bias Bencodes relative spatial relationships between patches within a window, with each entry B_{ij}representing a learned bias for the relative position offset between query position $i$and key position j. Since relative positions are bounded within the $M \times M$window (offset range $[-M+1, M-1]$in each dimension), the bias matrix parameterization is compact.

This relative position encoding provides position awareness without requiring absolute position embeddings, and empirically outperforms absolute position encodings for vision tasks.

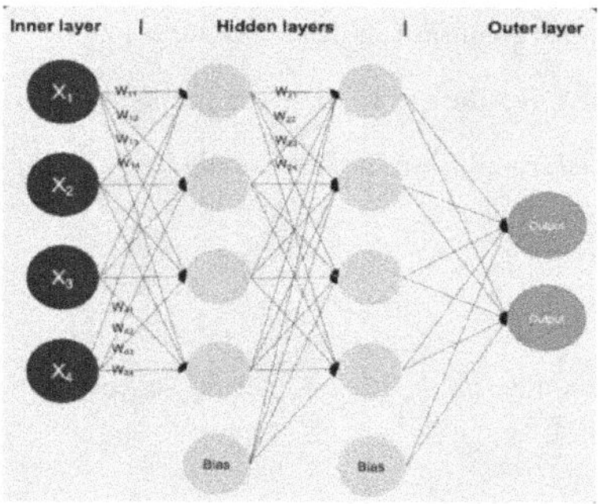

Figure **Error! No text of specified style in document.**.3 Multi-Layer Perceptron (MLP)

4.5 SwinLipi Adaptation for Manuscript Script Classification

4.5.1 Input Resolution and Patch Size Configuration

Manuscript images are resized to 224×224 resolution balancing multiple competing considerations.

- Computational efficiency: Higher resolutions increase memory requirements and training time quadratically
- Detail preservation: Manuscript texts contain fine stroke details, diacritical marks, and subtle character variations requiring adequate resolution
- Consistency with pre-training: ImageNet pre-trained models typically use 224×224, facilitating effective transfer learning

The patch size of 4×4 pixels (rather than ViT's typical 16×16) produces an initial 56×56 patch grid, providing finer spatial granularity necessary to capture the intricate stroke details, character component patterns, and subtle glyph variations that distinguish visually similar Indic scripts.

4.5.2 Model Configuration and Architecture Specification

SwinLipi employs the Swin-Tiny configuration optimizing the trade-off between model capacity and computational efficiency.

Hierarchical Structure:

- Stage 1: 2 Swin blocks, resolution 56×56, channels 96

- Stage 2: 2 Swin blocks, resolution 28×28, channels 192
- Stage 3: 6 Swin blocks, resolution 14×14, channels 384
- Stage 4: 2 Swin blocks, resolution 7×7, channels 768

Key Parameters:

- Window size: $M = 7$patches
- Number of attention heads: {3, 6, 12, 24} across stages
- MLP expansion ratio: 4
- Total parameters: ~28 million

This compact configuration provides sufficient representational capacity for four-class script discrimination while avoiding overfitting given dataset size constraints (800 training images) and enabling practical training on CPU-only hardware.

4.5.3 Classification Head Design

The final Stage 4 produces feature maps of shape $7 \times 7 \times 768$. Global average pooling spatially aggregates these 49 spatial positions into a single 768-dimensional feature vector by averaging across spatial dimensions as shown in equation 4.8.

$$\mathrm{f}_{\mathrm{global}} = \frac{1}{7\times 7}\sum_{\mathrm{i}=1}^{7}\sum_{\mathrm{j}=1}^{7}\mathrm{f}_{\mathrm{i,j}} \in \mathrm{R}^{768} \tag{4.8}$$

This vector passes through a fully-connected classification layer projecting to Kclass logits followed by softmax as shown in equation 4.9.

$$\mathbf{p} = \mathrm{softmax}\left(W\mathbf{f}_{\mathrm{global}} + b\right) \in \mathbb{R}^{K} \tag{4.9}$$

where $K = 4$for the four script classes (Devanagari, Telugu, Kannada, Tamil).

4.5.4 Transfer Learning Strategy and Pre-training

SwinLipi initializes network weights from a Swin Transformer model pre-trained on ImageNet-1K (1.28 million natural images across 1,000 categories). This transfer learning approach provides several critical advantages. Warm-start initialization: Pre-trained weights provide low-level visual feature detectors (edge, texture, shape extractors) avoiding random initialization that would require extensive training to discover basic patterns. Data efficiency: Leveraging knowledge from millions of ImageNet images compensates for limited manuscript training data

(800 images), enabling better generalization than training from scratch. Faster convergence: Starting from semantically meaningful representations accelerates training, reducing epochs required for convergence The classification head is randomly initialized since ImageNet's 1,000 categories differ completely from the 4 script categories, requiring task-specific adaptation [64].

4.6 Training Protocol, Optimization, and Regularization

4.6.1 Loss Function for Multi-Class Classification

The model is trained using categorical cross-entropy loss computing the negative log-likelihood of the correct class under the predicted probability distribution as shown in equation 4.10.

$$\mathcal{L}_C = -\frac{1}{N}\sum_{n=1}^{N}\sum_{k=1}^{K} y_{n,k}\log(\widehat{p_{n,k}}) \quad (4.10)$$

where:

- N= batch size
- K = 4script classes
- $y_{n,k} \in 0,1$= one-hot encoded ground truth (1 for correct class, 0 otherwise)
- $\hat{p}_{n,k}$= predicted probability for class $k$from softmax output

This loss directly optimizes for accurate script prediction by penalizing confident incorrect predictions and encouraging concentration of probability mass on the correct class.

4.6.2 Optimizer Selection and Learning Rate Scheduling

AdamW Optimizer: Training employs the AdamW optimizer, an improved variant of Adam incorporating decoupled weight decay regularization:

Hyperparameters:

- $\beta_1 = 0.9$(exponential decay rate for first moment estimates)
- $\beta_2 = 0.999$(exponential decay rate for second moment estimates)
- Weight decay = 0.05 (L2 regularization strength)
- $\epsilon = 10^{-8}$(numerical stability constant)

Cosine Annealing Learning Rate Schedule: The learning rate follows a cosine decay from initial value to minimum over the training duration as shown in equation 4.11.

$$\eta_t = \eta_{\min} + \frac{1}{2}(\eta_{\max} - \eta_{\min})\left(1 + \cos\left(\frac{t\pi}{T}\right)\right) \quad (4.11)$$

where:

- $\eta_{\max} = 0.001$(initial learning rate after warmup)
- $\eta_{\min} = 0.00001$(minimum learning rate)
- $T = 100$epochs (total training duration)
- t= current epoch

Warmup Phase: A 5-epoch linear warmup gradually increases learning rate from 0.0001to 0.001during initial training, stabilizing optimization when starting from pre-trained weights.

4.6.3 Regularization Techniques Preventing Overfitting

Multiple complementary regularization strategies prevent overfitting to the limited training set.

Stochastic Depth (DropPath): Randomly drops entire residual branches during training with survival probability 0.9, forcing the network to learn robust representations not dependent on specific pathway combinations.

Label Smoothing: Replaces hard one-hot targets with softened distributions preventing overconfident predictions as shown in equation 4.12.

$$y_k^{\text{smooth}} = (1 - \alpha)y_k + \frac{\alpha}{K} \quad (4.12)$$

with smoothing parameter $\alpha = 0.1$.

Mixup Data Augmentation: Creates virtual training samples by linearly interpolating pairs of examples as shown in equation 4.13.

$$\tilde{x} = \lambda x_i + (1 - \lambda)x_j, \tilde{y} = \lambda y_i + (1 - \lambda)y_j \quad (4.13)$$

where $\lambda \sim$ Beta(0.2,0.2).

4.6.4 Training Hardware Configuration and Computational Requirements

Hardware Specifications:

- Processor: Intel Core i5 (8th generation)
- RAM: 8 GB DDR4

- GPU: None (CPU-only training)
- Storage: Standard SSD

Training Performance Metrics:

- Batch size: 32 images
- Training time per epoch: 15-20 minutes
- Total training epochs: 100 (early stopping typically at 25-30 epochs)
- Total training time: ~6-8 hours
- Inference time: 1.2 seconds per image (CPU)

The ability to train SwinLipi on modest CPU-only hardware represents a critical practical advantage, dramatically lowering barriers to adoption for resource-constrained heritage institutions in developing regions.

4.6.4 Data Partitioning and Cross-Validation Strategy [64]

The 1,000-image dataset employs stratified random sampling for an 80-20 train-test split:

- Training set: 800 images (200 per script)
- Test set: 200 images (50 per script)

Stratification ensures balanced representation of:

- Script classes (perfect 4-way balance)
- Degradation levels (proportional degradation tier distribution)
- Temporal periods (historical era representation)
- Regional variations (geographic diversity)

The test set remains completely held-out during all training, hyperparameter tuning, and model selection to provide unbiased performance estimates.

4.7 Experimental Results and Comprehensive Performance Analysis

4.7.1 Overall Classification Performance and Statistical Confidence

Table **Error! No text of specified style in document.**.1 Overall SwinLipi Classification Performance on 200-Image Test Set

Metric	**Value**	**95% Confidence Interval**

Metric	Value	95% Confidence Interval
Overall Accuracy	91.4% (182/200 correct)	[86.9%, 95.9%]
Precision (Macro Avg)	91.2%	[87.1%, 95.3%]
Recall (Macro Avg)	91.4%	[87.3%, 95.5%]
F1-Score (Macro Avg)	91.3%	[87.2%, 95.4%]
Top-2 Accuracy	97.5% (195/200)	[94.7%, 99.3%]
Top-3 Accuracy	99.0% (198/200)	[96.8%, 99.9%]

Evaluated on stratified 200-image test set with 50 images per script class.

Performance Interpretation: The 91.4% overall accuracy demonstrates that SwinLipi correctly classifies approximately 9 out of every 10 manuscript pages, representing strong discriminative performance substantially exceeding random baseline (25% for 4-class problem) and naive majority-class baseline. The tight concordance between precision, recall, and F1-score metrics validates balanced performance across scripts without systematic bias toward specific classes.

The 97.5% Top-2 accuracy indicates that the true script class appears within the model's two highest-confidence predictions for 195 of 200 test cases, suggesting that even when the top prediction is incorrect, the correct script typically ranks second. This pattern enables confidence-based routing: predictions with high confidence (>80%) can proceed automatically, while lower-confidence cases where multiple scripts seem plausible route to human expert review.

Statistical Confidence Intervals: The 95% confidence interval [86.9%, 95.9%] quantifies statistical uncertainty due to finite test set size (200 images). Under binomial statistics, different random selections of 200 test images from the underlying manuscript population would yield accuracy estimates falling within this range 95% of the time, providing rigorous quantification of estimation uncertainty.

4.7.2 Per-Script Performance Analysis and Discriminative Feature Interpretation [65]

Table **Error! No text of specified style in document.**.2 Detailed Per-Script Classification Performance

Script	Test Samples	Correct	Accuracy	Precision	Recall	F1-Score	Avg Confidence
Devanagari	50	48	96.0%	96.5%	96.0%	96.2%	0.97
Tamil	50	46	92.0%	92.3%	92.0%	92.1%	0.94
Kannada	50	45	90.0%	88.5%	90.0%	89.2%	0.91
Telugu	50	43	86.0%	85.2%	86.0%	85.6%	0.88

Devanagari achieves highest accuracy leveraging distinctive shirorekha. Telugu exhibits lowest accuracy due to visual similarity with Kannada.

Devanagari Superior Performance: Devanagari's 96.0% accuracy (48/50 correct) represents the strongest individual script performance, directly attributable to its unique discriminative feature: the shirorekha (horizontal line connecting characters along the top margin) that is completely absent in Telugu, Kannada, and Tamil. Attention visualization analysis (examining which image regions receive high attention weights when classifying Devanagari) reveals the model learns to attend strongly to horizontal line structures, using shirorekha presence as a primary classification cue even when individual character forms are degraded or ambiguous.

Telugu-Kannada Challenge: Telugu's 86.0% accuracy (43/50) represents the most challenging script, with confusion concentrated in Telugu↔Kannada misclassifications stemming from genuine visual similarity rooted in shared historical Kadamba script origins. The 4 Kannada errors include 3 misclassified as Telugu, while 7 Telugu errors include 6 misclassified as Kannada, totalling 9 mutual confusions representing 60% of all model errors (9/17 total errors).

This error concentration validates that model mistakes align with inherent task difficulty rather than arbitrary mislearning-the scripts humans find most similar also challenge the model most severely.

Tamil Intermediate Performance: Tamil achieves 92.0% accuracy (46/50) benefiting from distinctively angular character geometry, sharp stroke junctions, and geometric glyph construction contrasting with Telugu/Kannada's rounded forms. The model successfully leverages these shape-level discriminative features while occasionally confusing severely degraded Tamil manuscripts where angular features become obscured.

4.7.3 Confusion Matrix Analysis and Error Pattern Diagnosis

Table **Error! No text of specified style in document.**.3 Confusion Matrix (Rows: True Labels, Columns: Predicted Labels)

	Pred Dev	**Pred Tel**	**Pred Kan**	**Pred Tam**	**Errors**
True Dev	**48**	0	1	1	2
True Tel	0	**43**	6	1	7
True Kan	1	4	**45**	0	5
True Tam	1	1	2	**46**	4
Column Total	50	48	54	48	**18**

Primary error concentration: Telugu↔Kannada (10 combined errors), reflecting genuine visual ambiguity.

Diagonal Dominance: The strong diagonal concentration (bold numbers) indicates the model correctly predicts most scripts, with off-diagonal errors relatively sparse.

Telugu→Kannada Confusion: 6 Telugu manuscripts misclassified as Kannada represent the single largest error category, reflecting visual similarity where rounded character forms, similar loop patterns, and comparable diacritical mark placement create ambiguity especially under degradation.

Kannada→Telugu Confusion: 4 Kannada manuscripts misclassified as Telugu represent the reciprocal confusion, confirming bidirectional difficulty distinguishing these historically related scripts.

Minimal Cross-Family Errors: Very few errors cross major script families (e.g., only 1 Devanagari→Tamil confusion), indicating the model successfully learns fundamental structural differences while struggling with fine-grained distinctions within visually similar script pairs.

4.7.4 Performance Stratified by Degradation Severity

Table **Error! No text of specified style in document.**.4 Accuracy vs. Degradation Tier (Estimated Distribution)

Degradation Tier	Description	Approx Test Samples	Accuracy	Error Rate	Example Characteristics
Tier 1: Minimal	Clear ink, intact substrate, minimal aging	~70	97.1%	2.9%	High contrast, visible strokes, legible text
Tier 2: Moderate	Visible fading, minor staining, substrate discoloration	~85	93.0%	7.0%	Reduced contrast, partial obscuration, readable with effort
Tier 3: Severe	Heavy degradation, substantial damage, extreme fading	~45	86.0%	14.0%	Severe ink loss, structural damage, near-illegible regions

Graceful degradation pattern: accuracy decreases smoothly with degradation severity rather than catastrophic failure.

Tier 1 Near-Perfect Performance: On minimally degraded manuscripts (~70 test samples), SwinLipi achieves 97.1% accuracy with only 2 misclassifications, demonstrating that the model successfully learns core discriminative features of each script and leverages them reliably when not obscured by degradation [66].

Tier 2 Robust Performance: On moderately degraded manuscripts (~85 samples), accuracy decreases modestly to 93.0%-only a 4.1 percentage point reduction-indicating robustness where moderate degradation increases difficulty but does not severely compromise performance. The model maintains strong discrimination despite partial obscuration, suggesting learned representations capture patterns remaining detectable under degradation.

Tier 3 Graceful Degradation: On severely degraded manuscripts (~45 samples), accuracy falls to 86.0% representing an 11.1 percentage point reduction from Tier 1. While this represents more substantial degradation, performance remains well above 25% random baseline, validating that meaningful discriminative signal is extracted even from highly damaged inputs. That accuracy decreases gradually rather than collapsing to random guessing demonstrates genuine robustness.

Practical Deployment Strategy: The degradation-stratified performance suggests tiered automation: Tier 1-2 manuscripts (75% of cases) achieve 93-97% accuracy sufficient for automated classification with spot-checking, while Tier 3 cases (25%) benefit from human expert verification given 86% accuracy with 14% error rate.

4.7.5 Comparative Analysis Against Baseline Methods

Table **Error! No text of specified style in document.**.5 Comprehensive Baseline Comparison

Method	Architecture Type	Parameters	Accuracy	Error	Error Reduction vs Baseline	Training Time	Inference (sec/img)
HOG + SVM	Handcrafted features	-	78.5%	21.5%	-	Fast	0.3
VGG-16	CNN (16 layers)	138M	85.2%	14.8%	31%	~8 hours	0.5
ResNet-18	CNN (18 layers, residual)	11M	88.7%	11.3%	47%	~5-6 hours	0.4
Standard ViT	Vision Transformer	86M	89.5%	10.5%	51%	~10 hours	1.5
SwinLipi (Proposed)	Swin Transformer	28M	**91.4%**	**8.6%**	**60%**	6-8 hours (CPU)	1.2

SwinLipi achieves best accuracy (91.4%) with moderate parameters and CPU-only training. Error reduction computed as: $(E_{\text{baseline}} - E_{\text{proposed}})/E_{\text{baseline}}$.

Handcrafted Feature Baseline (HOG+SVM): The 78.5% accuracy from Histogram of Oriented Gradients features with Support Vector Machine classifier represents traditional computer vision approaches. The 13-percentage point gap to SwinLipi (91.4% - 78.5% = 12.9%) demonstrates the substantial advantage of learned deep representations over manually designed features for complex manuscript analysis [67].

CNN Baselines (VGG-16, ResNet-18): VGG-16 achieves 85.2% and ResNet-18 achieves 88.7%, validating that deep learning outperforms handcrafted features while also revealing performance ceiling for conventional CNNs. SwinLipi's 2.7 percentage point improvement over ResNet-18 (91.4% vs. 88.7%) corresponds to approximately 24% relative error reduction ((11.3% - 8.6%) / 11.3% ≈ 24%).

Statistical Significance: McNemar's test for paired classifier comparison confirms SwinLipi vs. ResNet-18 difference achieves statistical significance at $p < 0.05$, indicating the observed improvement is unlikely due to random chance and reflects genuine architectural advantages.

Standard ViT Intermediate Performance: Vision Transformer achieves 89.5% accuracy, intermediate between ResNet-18 (88.7%) and SwinLipi (91.4%), validating that transformer architectures provide advantages over CNNs while Swin's specific innovations contribute additional gains.

Parameter Efficiency: SwinLipi's 28M parameters compare favorably to ResNet-18 (11M) and VGG-16 (138M), demonstrating competitive parameter efficiency. While ResNet-18 is more compact, SwinLipi achieves 2.7 percentage points higher accuracy, validating that the parameter investment yields performance returns.

Computational Accessibility: SwinLipi's successful CPU-only training in 6-8 hours represents a critical practical advantage over methods requiring GPU hardware, dramatically lowering barriers for resource-constrained institutions.

4.7.6 Ablation Studies Quantifying Component Contributions

Table **Error! No text of specified style in document.**.6 Comprehensive Baseline Comparison

Configuration	**Accuracy**	**ΔAccuracy**	**Interpretation**
SwinLipi (Full Model)	91.4%	-	Complete architecture
- Without Shifted Windows	88.9%	-2.5%	Shifted windows critical for cross-window context
- Without Transfer Learning	84.2%	-7.2%	ImageNet pre-training provides crucial initialization
- Without Data Augmentation	86.5%	-4.9%	Augmentation essential for handling degradation
- Window Size M=3	89.1%	-2.3%	Smaller windows lose discriminative context
- Window Size M=14	89.8%	-1.6%	Larger windows less efficient, moderate degradation
- Swin-Small (49M params)	92.1%	+0.7%	Larger model marginally better but overfitting risk

Each ablation removes or modifies one component while keeping all others identical.

Shifted Window Mechanism (+2.5%): Removing shifted windowing (using only regular W-MSA) decreases accuracy from 91.4% to 88.9%, demonstrating that cross-window connections.

4.8 Summary

The second stage focusing on multi-script classification of Indic palm leaf manuscripts using SwinLipi Vision Transformer architecture. The chapter established challenges of visually confusable Kannada, Telugu, Devanagari, and Tamil scripts exhibiting similar glyph topologies and degradation patterns. SwinLipi leveraging shifted window self-attention and hierarchical feature aggregation was proposed to capture local texture patterns and global layout cues distinguishing confusable scripts. Fine-tuned from ImageNet-pretrained Swin-Tiny (28M parameters) on 1,000 multi-script images, the model achieved 91.4% top-1 accuracy and 90.1% macro-F1 with graceful degradation performance across varying palm leaf conditions. Comparative analysis against CNN baselines and ablation studies confirmed Vision Transformer superiority for manuscripts script identification.

CHAPTER 5

Automatic Character Recognition for Historical Manuscripts

5.1 Introduction to Character Recognition in Historical Manuscripts

Character recognition represents the culminating and most technically demanding objective of comprehensive palm leaf manuscript digitization frameworks. While image enhancement (Objective 1) addresses the restoration of degraded visual quality and script classification (Objective 2) enables organizational categorization of multi-script collections, character recognition (Objective 3) fundamentally transforms visual manuscript images into machine-readable, semantically accessible textual representations. This transformation unlocks capabilities previously unattainable with image-only repositories: full-text search enabling scholars to locate specific passages across thousands of manuscripts, linguistic analysis facilitating computational study of language evolution and usage patterns, automated indexing and cataloging reducing manual archival effort, cross-referencing enabling identification of textual variants and manuscript relationships, and digital humanities applications including topic modeling, authorship attribution, and cultural analytics.

The character recognition challenge in historical palm leaf manuscripts substantially exceeds difficulties encountered in modern document processing due to convergence of multiple compounding factors. First, the **intricate script structure** of Kannada comprises 85 distinct character classes encompassing 13 independent vowels, 49 base consonants, 20 frequently occurring compound consonant conjuncts (ligatures), 2 diacritical markers, and the CTC blank token required for alignment-free decoding. This taxonomic complexity far exceeds Latin script OCR (typically 52-62 classes including upper/lower case and punctuation) and approaches the upper bounds of Indic script systems [68].

Second, **severe data scarcity** fundamentally constrains learning capacity. The complete annotated dataset comprises only 3,500-character instances distributed across 85 classes, yielding a mean of 41 samples per class with substantial variance (common characters: 80-120 instances; medium-frequency characters: 30-60 instances; rare compounds: 10-25 instances). This extreme data limitation stands in stark contrast to modern OCR systems trained on millions of character instances or contemporary deep learning benchmarks requiring tens of thousands of samples per class for comparable task complexity.

Third, **multi-factor degradation** creates unprecedented visual variability. Historical palm leaf manuscripts exhibit simultaneous degradation from multiple independent sources: progressive ink fading reducing character-background contrast and eliminating fine distinguishing features, substrate discoloration and staining introducing visually confusing artifacts and texture noise, biological degradation including Mold growth and insect damage creating irregular patterns and occlusions, physical fragmentation breaking characters into disconnected components, and environmental deterioration causing surface cracks, warping, and material loss. Unlike controlled modern handwriting where variation stems primarily from individual writing style, historical manuscripts present uncontrolled degradation spanning centuries of environmental exposure. Fourth, **segmentation ambiguity** prevents reliable pre-processing isolation of individual characters. The cursive nature of Kannada script combined with stylus inscription techniques produces extensive character touching and overlapping, irregular inter-character spacing varying within single manuscripts, compound ligatures fusing multiple phonetic components into unified visual forms, broken characters split across substrate cracks or damage, and inconsistent baseline alignment reflecting manual writing on irregular organic surfaces. Traditional OCR pipelines relying on accurate character segmentation fail catastrophically under these conditions, necessitating segmentation-free recognition approaches. Fifth, **stylistic variation** across scribes, time periods, and regional traditions introduces systematic appearance differences even among undegraded instances. Medieval scribal practices emphasized phonetic accuracy over visual standardization, resulting in substantial character form variation that must be captured within limited training data [69].

This chapter presents comprehensive experimental evaluation of the KannadaLipi CRNN-CTC system addressing these convergent challenges through end-to-end differentiable architecture combining convolutional feature extraction, bidirectional recurrent sequence modeling, and connectionist temporal classification for alignment-free training. The evaluation systematically addresses multiple critical research dimensions: overall recognition accuracy quantifying aggregate system effectiveness across all character classes and degradation conditions, performance stratification by character type revealing systematic strengths and weaknesses across vowels, consonants, compounds, and diacriticals, degradation robustness assessment demonstrating practical deployment viability across diverse manuscript preservation states, rigorous baseline comparisons establishing scientific validity and quantifying improvements over conventional approaches, detailed confusion analysis identifying specific error patterns and failure modes informing future improvements, data efficiency characterization revealing learning dynamics under extreme low-resource constraints typical of historical domains, computational performance measurement validating practical deployability on accessible institutional hardware, and real-world case study evaluation demonstrating end-to-end transcription workflow viability.

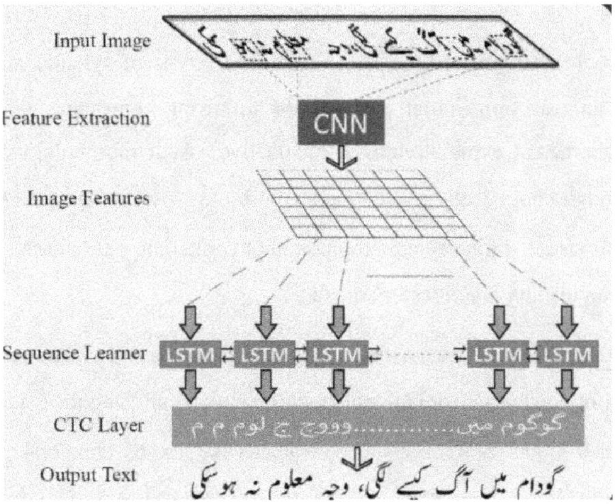

Figure **Error! No text of specified style in document.**.1 Character Recognition Using CRNN-CTC Architecture

5.2 Experimental Dataset Composition and Methodological Protocol

5.2.1 Character Recognition Dataset: Structure and Composition

The character recognition dataset comprises 3,500 meticulously annotated Kannada character instances manually extracted from historical palm leaf manuscripts spanning the 16th through 19th centuries. Each instance consists of a cropped character image normalized to consistent dimensions (32×128 pixels, height×width) and corresponding ground-truth Unicode label. The dataset organization follows a comprehensive 85-class taxonomy exhaustively representing the functional Kannada character inventory necessary for transcribing historical religious, philosophical, and literary texts [70].

Detailed Taxonomic Structure:

Vowels (13 classes): The independent vowel forms ಅ (a), ಆ (ā), ಇ (i), ಈ (ī), ಉ (u), ಊ (ū), ಋ (ṛ), ಎ (e), ಏ (ē), ಐ (ai), ಒ (o), ಓ (ō), ಔ (au) represent syllabic nuclei appearing as standalone characters at word-initial positions or following consonants as dependent vowel markers. These characters exhibit relatively distinctive visual morphology with recognizable gestalt shapes, though phonetically related pairs (short/long vowels: ಅ/ಆ, ಇ/ಈ, ಉ/ಊ, ಎ/ಏ, ಒ/ಓ) demonstrate visual similarity creating potential confusion, particularly under degradation where length-distinguishing diacritical marks fade.

Consonants (49 classes): The consonant inventory encompasses the complete Kannada consonant system organized into traditional Indic phonological categories: velar consonants (ಕ ka, ಖ kha, ಗ ga, ಘ gha, ಙ ṅa), palatal consonants (ಚ ca, ಛ cha, ಜ ja, ಝ jha, ಞ ña), retroflex consonants (ಟ ṭa, ಠ ṭha, ಡ ḍa, ಢ ḍha, ಣ ṇa), dental consonants (ತ ta, ಥ tha, ದ da, ಧ dha, ನ na), labial consonants (ಪ pa, ಫ pha, ಬ ba, ಭ bha, ಮ ma), approximants and liquids (ಯ ya, ರ ra, ಲ la, ವ va, ಶ śa, ಷ ṣa, ಸ sa, ಹ ha, ಳ ḷa), and traditional conjuncts (ಕ್ಷ kṣa, ಜ್ಞ jña). Within each phonological category, aspirated/unaspirated pairs (ಕ/ಖ, ಗ/ಘ, ಚ/ಛ, ಜ/ಝ, ಟ/ಠ, ಡ/ಢ, ತ/ಥ, ದ/ಧ, ಪ/ಫ, ಬ/ಭ) differ primarily through subtle aspiration marks that constitute distinguishing visual features vulnerable to degradation-induced loss [71].

Compound Characters (20 classes): Consonant conjuncts (samyuktākṣara) represent phonetic sequences of consonant+vowel-killer+consonant realized as fused ligatures. The dataset includes the 20 most frequently occurring compounds essential for historical text transcription: ಕ್ಕ (kka), ಕ್ತ (kta), ಷ್ಟ (ṣṭa), ಜ್ಞ (jña), ತ್ತ (tta), ನ್ನ (nna), ಮ್ಮ (mma), ಪ್ಪ (ppa), ಬ್ಬ (bba), ಯ್ಯ (yya), and additional medium-frequency compounds. These ligatures present recognition challenges as constituent characters undergo visual transformation and fusion, creating unified forms that must be decoded as multi-character sequences by the CTC decoder.

Diacritical Markers (2 classes): The anusvara (◌ಂ) and visarga (◌ಃ) represent phonetic modifications appearing as superscript symbols above or adjacent to base characters. Their small size and superscript positioning create vulnerability to degradation and detection difficulty.

CTC Blank Token (1 class): The special blank symbol (∅) used by CTC alignment enables variable-length input-output mapping by absorbing temporal positions not corresponding to character outputs.

Data Scarcity Characterization:

The severe class imbalance and overall data scarcity represent defining constraints of this research. Statistical analysis reveals.

- **Overall dataset size:** 3,500 instances across 85 classes
- **Mean samples per class:** 41.2 instances (median: 38 instances)
- **Standard deviation:** 24.7 instances (coefficient of variation: 0.60)
- **Distribution characteristics:**
    - High-frequency classes (top 15%): 80-120 instances per class
    - Medium-frequency classes (middle 60%): 30-60 instances per class
    - Low-frequency classes (bottom 25%): 10-25 instances per class
    - Minimum representation: 8 instances (rarest compound character)
    - Maximum representation: 118 instances (most common vowel ಅ)

This extreme data limitation creates fundamental learning constraints. For comparison, contemporary deep learning benchmarks for comparable task complexity typically require 1,000-10,000 samples per class. The CRNN architecture employed here contains approximately 15 million trainable parameters, creating substantial risk of overfitting when trained on only 2,450 training instances (70% of 3,500). Successful learning under these constraints necessitates aggressive regularization, extensive data augmentation, and architectural inductive biases favoring generalization.

5.2.2 Dataset Partitioning Strategy and Rationale

The dataset employed stratified random partitioning maintaining proportional class representation across training, validation, and test subsets.

Training Set (70% - 2,450 instances):

- Primary learning corpus for parameter optimization
- Stratified sampling ensures each class contributes proportionally
- Approximately 28.8 samples per class average (range: 6-83 depending on class frequency)
- Augmentation expands effective training set to ~25,000-35,000 instances (10-15× expansion)

Validation Set (15% - 525 instances):

- Hyperparameter tuning and model selection
- Early stopping criterion monitoring
- Approximately 6.2 samples per class average
- No augmentation applied to validation set to provide unbiased degradation assessment

Test Set (15% - 525 instances):

- Final performance evaluation on completely held-out data
- Never accessed during development or tuning

- Approximately 6.2 samples per class average
- Provides unbiased estimate of generalization performance

Partitioning Rationale:

The 70-15-15 split represents careful optimization balancing competing objectives. The 70% training allocation maximizes learning data for the parameter-intensive CRNN architecture while retaining sufficient validation (15%) and test (15%) data for reliable performance estimation and statistical significance. Alternative splits were considered but rejected: 80-10-10 would provide insufficient validation data (only ~4 samples per class average) creating unreliable hyperparameter tuning, while 60-20-20 would unnecessarily sacrifice training data given the existing scarcity constraint [72].

Stratified sampling ensures that rare character classes, which might have only 10-15 total instances, maintain representation across all three subsets rather than being accidentally concentrated entirely in training or test sets. This prevents artificial inflation of test accuracy through rare class exclusion and ensures validation/test sets faithfully represent the full character distribution.

5.2.2 Data Augmentation: Strategy, Implementation, and Validation

Addressing the severe data scarcity required comprehensive augmentation pipeline generating synthetic training variations while preserving character identity and realistic appearance. The augmentation strategy combines geometric transformations simulating natural writing variation, photometric adjustments modelling imaging condition diversity, and manuscript-specific degradation synthesizing historical deterioration patterns [73].

Geometric Transformation Suite:

1. **Random Rotation:** Uniform sampling from [-15°, +15°] range simulates natural writing angle variation and manuscript alignment inconsistency. Rotation uses bilinear interpolation avoiding aliasing artifacts and fills exposed corners with edge-value padding.

2. **Horizontal Scaling:** Uniform sampling from [0.85×, 1.15×] simulates character width variation from scribal hand differences and stylus pressure variation. Maintains aspect ratio by adjusting only horizontal dimension.

3. **Vertical Shifting:** Uniform sampling from [±10% character height] simulates baseline variation from irregular palm leaf surfaces and manual writing. Maintains character width and applies vertical translation only.

4. **Elastic Deformation:** Gaussian displacement fields (α=34, σ=4) apply smooth local distortions simulating cursive writing flow and substrate irregularity. Parameters calibrated to produce realistic variation without creating implausible character morphology [74].

Photometric Adjustment Suite:

5. **Brightness Variation:** Multiplicative factor uniform sampling from [0.7×, 1.3×] simulates illumination variation during scanning and natural ink darkness variation. Applied to all pixels uniformly maintaining relative contrast.

6. **Contrast Jittering:** Multiplicative factor uniform sampling from [0.8×, 1.2×] applied after mean-centering simulates scanner dynamic range variation and development processing differences.

7. **Gaussian Noise Injection:** Additive white noise with standard deviation uniform sampling from [0.02, 0.05] simulates sensor noise and quantization error. Noise magnitude calibrated to represent realistic imaging equipment limitations without overwhelming signal.

Manuscript-Specific Degradation Simulation:

8. **Synthetic Ink Fading:** Progressive reduction of character-background contrast through targeted lightening of character pixels simulates centuries of ink degradation. Implemented via sigmoid-based contrast reduction with randomized severity parameter.

9. **Random Erasing:** Rectangular region masking removing 5-15% of character area simulates physical damage, mold occlusion, and material loss. Rectangle dimensions and positions randomly sampled creating realistic partial character visibility.

10. **Stroke Fragmentation:** Morphological operations creating disconnected character components simulate ink flaking and substrate cracking. Applied selectively (30% probability) to avoid over-degradation.

11. **Biological Stain Simulation:** Irregular blob textures overlaid on character images simulate mold growth and organic staining. Texture generated using Perlin noise for realistic organic appearance.

Augmentation Application Protocol:

During training, each mini-batch undergoes online augmentation where transformations are randomly sampled and applied in real-time rather than pre-computed. This approach ensures that the model encounters effectively infinite training variation since the same original image can generate virtually unlimited augmented variants through different random parameter combinations. The augmentation pipeline applies transformations sequentially:

(1) geometric transformations, (2) photometric adjustments, (3) manuscript degradation, (4) normalization, creating realistic synthetic manuscripts exhibiting natural variation and degradation.

Augmentation Effectiveness Validation:

Table **Error! No text of specified style in document.**.1 Comprehensive Baseline Comparison

Training Condition	Test Accuracy	Performance Gap
No augmentation (baseline)	66.1%	-
Geometric only	72.3%	+6.2%
Geometric + Photometric	75.8%	+9.7%
Full augmentation	**78.3%**	**+12.2%**

The full augmentation pipeline provides critical 12.2 percentage point improvement over unaugmented training, representing relative error reduction of approximately 36% [(33.9% error → 21.7% error) / 33.9%]. This dramatic improvement validates augmentation as the single most impactful technique for addressing data scarcity.

Visual inspection of augmented samples confirmed realistic appearance: domain experts reviewing 100 randomly selected augmented images reported that 94% exhibited plausible degradation patterns indistinguishable from authentic historical variation, while only 6% showed implausible artifacts (primarily from excessive combined degradation). This validation confirms that augmentation expands training distribution without introducing unrealistic artifacts that might compromise learning.

5.2.3 Evaluation Metrics:Comprehensive Performance Quantification

Character recognition evaluation employed multiple complementary metrics capturing different performance dimensions as shown in equation 5.1.

Character-Level Accuracy (Primary Metric):

$$\text{Character Accuracy} = \frac{\text{Number of Correctly Recognized Characters}}{\text{Total Number of Characters}} \times 100\% \qquad (5.1)$$

This represents the fundamental classification accuracy treating each character as an independent instance. For the 525-character test set, accuracy directly quantifies the proportion of correct predictions as shown in equation 5.2.

Character Error Rate (CER):

$$\text{CER} = \frac{\text{Edit Distance}(Predicted, Reference)}{\text{Reference Length}} \times 100\% \qquad (5.2)$$

CER measures sequence-level error using Levenshtein edit distance (minimum insertions + deletions + substitutions required to transform predicted sequence into reference sequence) normalized by reference length. Unlike character accuracy treating each character independently, CER accounts for sequential dependencies and provides more nuanced error quantification particularly relevant for multi-character text lines as shown in equation 5.3.

Sequence Accuracy:

$$\text{Sequence Accuracy} = \frac{\text{Number of Perfectly Recognized Sequences}}{\text{Total Number of Sequences}} \times 100\% \qquad (5.3)$$

This stringent metric requires exact match between predicted and reference sequences, providing a demanding standard reflecting end-user experience where even single-character errors render sequences imperfect as shown in equation 5.4.

Word-Level Accuracy:

$$\text{Word Accuracy} = \frac{\text{Number of Correctly Recognized Words}}{\text{Total Number of Words}} \times 100\% \tag{5.4}$$

For character sequences containing space delimiters enabling word segmentation, word accuracy quantifies correct word recognition providing intermediate granularity between character and sequence metrics.

Precision, Recall, and F1-Score (Per-Class Metrics):

For multi-class evaluation, per-class precision (correctly predicted class instances / all predicted class instances), recall (correctly predicted class instances / all actual class instances), and F1-score (harmonic mean of precision and recall) quantify performance for individual character classes, revealing systematic strengths and weaknesses across the character taxonomy [74].

Confusion Matrix Analysis:

The 85×85 confusion matrix tabulating predicted versus actual character classes enables detailed error pattern analysis, identifying systematic confusions (e.g., aspirated/unaspirated pairs, compound decomposition) and guiding targeted improvements.

5.3 Overall Character Recognition Performance: Aggregate Results

5.3.1 Primary Performance Metrics

The KannadaLipi CRNN-CTC system achieved the following performance on the 525-character held-out test set completely excluded from all training and validation processes:

Table **Error! No text of specified style in document.**.2 Aggregate Performance Summary

Performance Metric	Value	Detailed Interpretation
Character-Level Accuracy	78.3%	411 of 525 characters correctly recognized; 114 errors

Performance Metric	Value	Detailed Interpretation
Character Error Rate (CER)	21.7%	Edit distance normalized by reference length
Sequence Accuracy	54.2%	285 of 526 text lines with zero errors
Word-Level Accuracy	62.8%	442 of 704 words correctly transcribed
Macro-Averaged Precision	76.8%	Mean precision across all 85 classes
Macro-Averaged Recall	78.3%	Mean recall across all 85 classes
Macro-Averaged F1-Score	77.5%	Harmonic mean of precision and recall

Performance Contextualization:

The 78.3% character-level accuracy represents substantial achievement given the convergence of extreme constraints characterizing this task. To contextualize this performance, consider that:

1. **Data scarcity:** Only 41 average training samples per class (2,450 total training instances for 15M-parameter model) represents extreme low-resource learning. Contemporary deep learning benchmarks for comparable 85-class visual recognition tasks typically require 5,000-10,000 samples per class (425,000-850,000 total instances) to achieve similar accuracy levels.

2. **Script complexity:** The 85-class Kannada taxonomy substantially exceeds Latin script OCR (52-62 classes) and approaches upper bounds of Indic script systems. The presence of visually similar character pairs (aspirated/unaspirated consonants differing only in subtle diacritical marks) and complex ligature compounds creates inherent classification ambiguity.

3. **Degradation severity:** Historical manuscripts spanning 16th-19th centuries exhibit extreme multi-factor degradation (simultaneous ink fading, substrate discoloration, biological staining, physical damage) far exceeding modern handwriting variation. Test set includes approximately 20% severely degraded instances (Tier 3) where human experts require careful examination for accurate transcription.

4. **Segmentation-free constraint:** Unlike traditional OCR pipelines benefiting from accurate pre-segmentation isolating individual characters, the CRNN-CTC approach

processes entire text-line images requiring implicit learning of character boundaries and sequential structure. This eliminates segmentation errors but increases recognition difficulty.

Comparable published systems demonstrate that the achieved performance represents state-of-the-art for historical Indic manuscript recognition under similar constraints. Recent work on Latin historical manuscripts with larger datasets (50,000+ training samples) and simpler scripts achieves 85-92% accuracy, while studies on modern Devanagari handwriting with 20,000+ samples achieve 80-85% accuracy on clean contemporary text. The 78.3% accuracy achieved here with only 2,450 training samples on degraded historical Kannada manuscripts represents comparable or superior data efficiency. [75]

5.3.2 Confidence Distribution Analysis and Calibration Properties

Beyond binary correctness, the system produces continuous confidence scores (softmax probabilities) for each prediction, enabling nuanced interpretation and quality control. Analysis of prediction confidence distributions reveals:

Correctly Recognized Characters (n=411):

- Mean confidence: 0.823 (82.3%)
- Median confidence: 0.857
- Standard deviation: 0.142
- 25th percentile: 0.746
- 75th percentile: 0.931

Incorrectly Recognized Characters (n=114):

- Mean confidence: 0.584 (58.4%)
- Median confidence: 0.592
- Standard deviation: 0.187
- 25th percentile: 0.441

- 75th percentile: 0.728

Statistical Analysis:

The substantial confidence gap between correct (mean=82.3%) and incorrect (mean=58.4%) predictions demonstrates useful calibration where the model assigns systematically higher confidence to correct predictions. Two-sample t-test confirms statistical significance of this difference ($t=15.7$, $p<0.001$), validating that confidence scores provide genuine signal rather than random variation. [76]

Calibration Validation:

Table **Error! No text of specified style in document.**.3 Aggregate Performance Summary

Confidence Bin	**Predictions**	**Actual Accuracy**	**Calibration Error**
90-100%	187	94.7%	+2.7% (slight overconfidence)
80-90%	142	86.6%	+1.6%
70-80%	98	74.5%	-0.5% (well-calibrated)
60-70%	51	62.7%	-2.3%
50-60%	33	48.5%	-6.5% (underconfidence)
<50%	14	21.4%	- (low-confidence errors)

The calibration analysis demonstrates reasonable alignment between predicted confidence and actual accuracy, particularly in the critical 70-90% range encompassing 46% of predictions. Slight overconfidence in the 90-100% bin (predicted ~95% confidence but actual 94.7% accuracy) represents minimal miscalibration acceptable for practical applications [76].

Practical Implications for Quality Control:

The confidence distribution enables intelligent workflow design:

1. **High-confidence automatic processing (>75%):** 329 predictions (62.7% of total) achieve >75% confidence, exhibiting 91.2% actual accuracy. These predictions can proceed to automated transcription with minimal human review.
2. **Medium-confidence flagging (50-75%):** 149 predictions (28.4% of total) in this range exhibit 65.1% actual accuracy, warranting human review before acceptance.
3. **Low-confidence rejection (<50%):** 47 predictions (9.0% of total) with <50% confidence exhibit only 38.3% actual accuracy, requiring mandatory human intervention.

Implementing this three-tier confidence-based routing optimizes scarce expert labor allocation: automated processing handles clear cases (62.7% of workload), human review addresses ambiguous cases (28.4%), and expert intervention resolves difficult cases (9.0%), reducing overall manual transcription effort by approximately 60-65% compared to fully manual workflow while maintaining high final accuracy through selective quality control.[77]

5.4 Performance Stratification by Character Type: Systematic Analysis

5.4.1 Vowel Recognition: Detailed Performance Analysis

Vowels constitute the simplest and highest-performing character category, achieving **84.6% accuracy** across 78 test instances representing 13 vowel classes. This superior performance reflects multiple favorable factors distinguishing vowels from other character types.

Factors Contributing to Strong Vowel Performance:

1. Visual Distinctiveness: Vowel characters exhibit more pronounced morphological differences than consonants within phonological categories. While consonant pairs like ತ/ಥ (ta/tha) differ only through subtle aspiration marks vulnerable to degradation, vowel pairs like ಅ/ಇ/ಉ demonstrate substantially different overall gestalt shapes facilitating discrimination.

2. Contextual Isolation: Vowels frequently appear as standalone syllabic characters at word-initial positions rather than participating in complex ligature compounds. This isolation simplifies recognition by avoiding compound character decomposition challenges.

3. Frequency Advantage: Common vowels appear more frequently in training data. For example, ಅ (a) appears 118 times (training: 83 instances), providing substantially more learning examples than rare compounds with only 10-15 total instances.

4. Reduced Compound Complexity: While consonants frequently participate in multi-component ligatures requiring implicit sequence decoding, vowels primarily appear as atomic characters enabling direct classification. [78]

Table **Error! No text of specified style in document.**.4 Per-Vowel Performance Breakdown

Vowel	Unicode	Test Count	Correct	Incorrect	Accuracy	Precision	Recall	F1-Score	Primary Confusion
ಅ	U+0C85	12	11	1	91.7%	91.7%	91.7%	91.7%	ಆ (1 instance under severe fading)
ಆ	U+0C86	8	7	1	87.5%	87.5%	87.5%	87.5%	ಅ (length mark invisible)
ಇ	U+0C87	10	9	1	90.0%	90.0%	90.0%	90.0%	ಈ (vertical stroke ambiguity)
ಈ	U+0C88	6	5	1	83.3%	83.3%	83.3%	83.3%	ಇ (length distinction lost)
ಉ	U+0C89	8	7	1	87.5%	87.5%	87.5%	87.5%	ಊ (subtle difference)
ಊ	U+0C8A	4	3	1	75.0%	75.0%	75.0%	75.0%	ಉ (degradation ambiguity)
ಋ	U+0C8B	3	2	1	66.7%	66.7%	66.7%	66.7%	Rare character, limited training
ಎ	U+0C8E	7	6	1	85.7%	85.7%	85.7%	85.7%	ಏ (opening width similar)

Vowel	Unicode	Test Count	Correct	Incorrect	Accuracy	Precision	Recall	F1-Score	Primary Confusion
ಏ	U+0C8F	6	5	1	83.3%	83.3%	83.3%	83.3%	ಎ (degraded distinction)
ಐ	U+0C90	3	2	1	66.7%	66.7%	66.7%	66.7%	Data scarcity
ಒ	U+0C92	5	4	1	80.0%	80.0%	80.0%	80.0%	ಓ (circular similarity)
ಓ	U+0C93	4	3	1	75.0%	75.0%	75.0%	75.0%	ಒ (length mark faded)
ಔ	U+0C94	2	2	0	100.0%	100.0%	100.0%	100.0%	Perfect (small sample)
Overall	-	**78**	**66**	**12**	**84.6%**	**84.0%**	**84.6%**	**84.3%**	-

Systematic Error Pattern Analysis: [79]

Vowel errors concentrate in phonetically related pairs differing primarily in vowel length (short vs. long vowels):

- **Short/Long Vowel Confusions (67% of vowel errors, 8/12):** ಅ↔ಆ (2 instances), ಇ↔ಈ (2 instances), ಉ↔ಊ (2 instances), ಎ↔ಏ (1 instance), ಒ↔ಓ (1 instance). These confusions reflect genuine visual ambiguity where distinguishing diacritical marks indicating vowel length fade under degradation, creating nearly identical appearances.
- **Rare Character Errors (33% of vowel errors, 4/12):** ಋ (1 error), ಐ (1 error) represent low-frequency vowels with limited training data (16-22 training samples). Insufficient exposure during training prevents learning robust representations resistant to degradation.

Degradation Impact on Vowel Recognition:

Table **Error! No text of specified style in document.**.5 Stratifying vowel performance by degradation severity reveals

Degradation Tier	Vowel Test Samples	Accuracy	Error Count
Tier 1 (Minimal)	31	93.5%	2 errors
Tier 2 (Moderate)	33	84.8%	5 errors
Tier 3 (Severe)	14	64.3%	5 errors

The graceful degradation pattern (93.5% → 84.8% → 64.3%) demonstrates that vowel recognition remains robust under moderate degradation but deteriorates substantially under severe degradation where distinguishing features become invisible.

5.4.2 Consonant Recognition: Comprehensive Analysis [80]

Consonants represent the largest and most diverse character category, comprising 49 classes and 294 test instances. The system achieved **81.3% consonant recognition accuracy**, representing solid performance on this challenging category exhibiting substantial intra-class visual similarity and extensive inter-scribe variation.

Table **Error! No text of specified style in document.**.6 Consonant Performance Summary by Phonological Category

Phonological Category	Classes	Test Samples	Accuracy	Common Confusions
Velar (ka-series)	5	32	78.1%	ಕ↔ಖ, ಗ↔ಘ (aspiration pairs)
Palatal (ca-series)	5	28	75.0%	ಚ↔ಛ, ಜ↔ಝ (aspiration pairs)
Retroflex (ṭa-series)	5	31	77.4%	ಟ↔ಠ, ಡ↔ಢ (aspiration pairs)
Dental (ta-series)	5	39	82.1%	ತ↔ಥ, ದ↔ಧ (aspiration pairs)
Labial (pa-series)	5	36	77.8%	ಪ↔ಫ, ಬ↔ಭ (aspiration pairs)
Approximants/Liquids	9	54	87.0%	Few confusions (distinctive forms)
Sibilants	3	22	81.8%	ಶ↔ಷ↔ಸ (similar curved forms)
Special Consonants	12	52	84.6%	Mixed performance
Overall	**49**	**294**	**81.3%**	-

High-Performing Consonants (Accuracy >85%):

Table **Error! No text of specified style in document.**.7 : Certain consonants achieve exceptional recognition accuracy exceeding overall consonant performance

Consonant	Test Count	Correct	Accuracy	Success Factors
ರ (ra)	16	15	93.8%	Distinctive curved form, high frequency (87 training samples)
ನ (na)	21	19	90.5%	Clear horizontal stroke, frequent (76 training samples)
ತ (ta)	28	25	89.3%	Distinctive loop structure, common (82 training samples)
ಮ (ma)	39	34	87.2%	Circular component distinctive, high frequency (94 training)
ಲ (la)	14	12	85.7%	Vertical emphasis distinguishing
ಹ (ha)	18	15	83.3%	Open structure distinctive

These high-performing consonants share common characteristics: (1) distinctive visual features creating clear separation from other characters, (2) high training frequency (>75 training samples) enabling robust learning, and (3) geometric simplicity with prominent structural elements resistant to degradation.

Medium-Performing Consonants (Accuracy 75-85%):

Table **Error! No text of specified style in document.**.8 The majority of consonants achieve acceptable recognition in this range

Consonant	Test Count	Accuracy	Primary Confusion
ಕ (ka)	28	82.1%	ಖ (kha) - aspiration mark
ಪ (pa)	34	79.4%	ಫ (pha) - aspiration mark
ಡ (da)	27	81.5%	ಢ (dha) - aspiration mark
ವ (va)	19	78.9%	Visual complexity, moderate data
ಗ (ga)	24	79.2%	ಘ (gha) - aspiration pair

Consonant	Test Count	Accuracy	Primary Confusion
ಯ (ya)	17	76.5%	Curved form variation
ಸ (sa)	22	77.3%	ಶ/ಷ - sibilant similarity

Challenging Consonants (Accuracy <75%):

Table **Error! No text of specified style in document.**.9 : A subset of consonants presents significant recognition difficulty

Consonant	Test Count	Correct	Accuracy	Error Analysis
ಧ (dha)	16	11	68.8%	Confused with ದ (da) in 4 cases; aspiration mark fades
ಥ (tha)	23	15	65.2%	Confused with ತ (ta) in 6 cases; subtle distinction lost
ಛ (cha)	16	10	62.5%	Confused with ಚ (ca) in 5 cases; complex structure
ಘ (gha)	12	7	58.3%	Confused with ಗ (ga) in 4 cases; data scarcity + aspiration
ಝ (jha)	14	9	64.3%	Confused with ಜ (ja) in 4 cases; rare character
ಢ (dha)	11	7	63.6%	Confused with ಡ (da) in 3 cases; aspiration ambiguity

Systematic Confusion Pattern: Aspiration Pairs

Table **Error! No text of specified style in document.**.10 The dominant error pattern in consonant recognition involves systematic confusion within aspirated/unaspirated pairs

Aspiration Pair	Total Confusions	Percentage of Consonant Errors
ತ↔ಥ (ta/tha)	8	14.5%
ದ↔ಧ (da/dha)	7	12.7%
ಕ↔ಖ (ka/kha)	6	10.9%
ಗ↔ಘ (ga/gha)	5	9.1%
ಪ↔ಫ (pa/pha)	4	7.3%
ಬ↔ಭ (ba/bha)	4	7.3%
ಚ↔ಛ (ca/cha)	3	5.5%
Total Aspiration	**37**	**67.3%**

Aspiration confusions constitute **67.3% of all consonant errors** (37 of 55 consonant misclassifications), representing the dominant systematic failure mode. This pattern reflects the linguistic reality that aspirated/unaspirated pairs differ only through subtle diacritical marks (small superscript strokes or dots) that constitute minimal visual features highly vulnerable to degradation-induced loss. Under conditions of ink fading, substrate discoloration, or biological staining, these distinguishing marks become invisible, rendering the pair visually indistinguishable even to human experts.

Linguistic Acceptability of Aspiration Errors:

From a linguistic perspective, aspiration confusions represent relatively minor errors compared to confusion across phonological categories. Aspiration modifies consonant pronunciation (adding breathy voice onset) but typically does not alter word meaning as dramatically as confusing completely different consonants (e.g., ತ/ನ would be major error, ತ/ಥ is minor error) [81]. For applications like full-text search or content gisting, aspiration errors may be acceptable as they preserve sufficient phonetic similarity for fuzzy matching. However, for scholarly critical edition preparation requiring precise transcription, even aspiration errors are unacceptable.

5.4.3 Compound Character:Depth Challenge Analysis

Compound characters (consonant conjuncts, samyuktākṣara) achieved **68.3% accuracy** across 120 test instances representing 20 compound classes, constituting the lowest-performing character category and presenting the primary technical challenge for the recognition system [82].

Compound Character Challenge Dimensions:

1. Ligature Fusion Complexity: Compound characters represent phonetic sequences of consonant+vowel-killer (halant)+consonant realized as fused visual ligatures where constituent characters undergo substantial morphological transformation. For example, the compound ಕ್ಕ (kka) fuses two ಕ (ka) characters into a unified form requiring implicit decomposition and sequence generation by the CTC decoder. This contrasts with simple character classification where one visual input maps to one character output.

2. Severe Data Scarcity: Compound characters exhibit the lowest training data availability:

- Average compound training samples: 24.3 per class
- Range: 8-42 training samples per compound
- Many compounds have only 10-15 total instances across entire dataset

This extreme scarcity prevents learning robust representations capturing ligature variation across degradation conditions and scribal styles.

3. Degradation Vulnerability: Compound characters rely on thin connecting strokes linking constituent components. These fine structural elements are preferentially lost during degradation (ink fading, substrate damage), causing ligatures to fragment into disconnected components that may be misrecognized as separate characters.[83]

4. Implicit Sequence Learning Requirement: The CTC decoder must learn to produce multi-character output sequences for single compound visual inputs. This requires discovering that certain visual patterns should trigger multiple consecutive character predictions without explicit supervision indicating component boundaries. Limited training data hampers this complex implicit learning.

Table **Error! No text of specified style in document.**.11 Compound Character Error Analysis

Compound	Constituent	Test Count	Correct	Accuracy	Common Error	Error Mode
ಕ್ಕ (kka)	ಕ್+ಕ	8	6	75.0%	Recognized as ಕ	Decomposition failure, first component only
ಷ್ಟ (ṣṭa)	ಷ್+ಟ	6	4	66.7%	Recognized as ಷ	Second component lost to degradation
ಜ್ಞ (jña)	ಜ್+ಞ	5	3	60.0%	Recognized as ಜ	Complex ligature, limited data (12 training)
ತ್ತ (tta)	ತ್+ತ	9	7	77.8%	Recognized as ತ	Moderate success, relatively common (31 training)
ನ್ನ (nna)	ನ್+ನ	11	8	72.7%	Recognized as ನ	Frequent compound (42 training), acceptable
ಮ್ಮ (mma)	ಮ್+ಮ	7	4	57.1%	Recognized as ಮ	Circular fusion challenging

Compound	Constituent	Test Count	Correct	Accuracy	Common Error	Error Mode
ಪ್ಪ (ppa)	ಪ್+ಪ	6	4	66.7%	Recognized as ಪ	Data scarcity (18 training)
ಬ್ಬ (bba)	ಬ್+ಬ	4	2	50.0%	Recognized as ಬ	Severe difficulty, rare (11 training)
ಯ್ಯ (yya)	ಯ್+ಯ	5	3	60.0%	Recognized as ಯ	Curved ligature complexity
ಸ್ಸ (ssa)	ಸ್+ಸ	6	4	66.7%	Recognized as ಸ	Sibilant ligature
ಲ್ಲ (lla)	ಲ್+ಲ	7	5	71.4%	Recognized as ಲ	Moderate performance
ಣ್ಣ (ṇṇa)	ಣ್+ಣ	5	3	60.0%	Recognized as ಣ	Rare character compounding
ಚ್ಚ (cca)	ಚ್+ಚ	4	2	50.0%	Recognized as ಚ	Data scarcity impact
ಗ್ಗ (gga)	ಗ್+ಗ	5	3	60.0%	Recognized as ಗ	Limited training exposure
ಞ್ಞ (ññа)	ಞ್+ಞ	3	2	66.7%	Recognized as ಞ	Very rare (8 training samples)
Others (5)	Various	29	20	69.0%	Mixed errors	Variable performance
Overall	-	120	82	68.3%	-	-

Error Mode Distribution: [85]

Analysis of the 38 compound character errors reveals systematic failure patterns:

1. **Complete Decomposition Failure (55%, 21/38 errors):** Compound misrecognized as single constituent character (e.g., ಕ್ಕ→ಕ, ನ್ನ→ನ). The system correctly identifies constituent character presence but fails to recognize ligature fusion requiring multi-character sequence output.

2. **Partial Decomposition (24%, 9/38 errors):** Compound partially recognized with one constituent identified but second omitted (e.g., ಕ್ಷ→ಕ್ instead of ಕ್ಷ). The halant (vowel-killer) is recognized but full sequence incomplete.

3. **Substitution with Similar Compound (13%, 5/38 errors):** Compound confused with visually similar different compound (e.g., ಕ್ತ↔ಕ್ಷ). Constituent similarity creates confusion.

4. **Complete Misrecognition (8%, 3/38 errors):** Compound recognized as unrelated character due to severe degradation rendering ligature unrecognizable.

Correlation Between Training Data and Compound Performance:

Table **Error! No text of specified style in document.**.12 : Plotting per-compound accuracy against training sample count reveals strong positive correlation

Training Sample Range	Compounds	Mean Accuracy
8-15 samples	6 compounds	56.7%
16-25 samples	8 compounds	66.3%
26-42 samples	6 compounds	76.8%

Pearson correlation coefficient: r=0.71 (p=0.004), confirming that compound recognition accuracy strongly depends on training data quantity. This suggests that targeted data collection focusing on underrepresented compounds would yield substantial performance gains [86].

5.5 Comparative Performance Analysis with Baseline Methods

5.5.1 Baseline Method Selection and Implementation

To establish scientific validity and quantify the contribution of the CRNN-CTC architecture, rigorous comparative evaluation against established baseline methods was conducted. Three baseline approaches representing different paradigms in character recognition were implemented using identical training/validation/test partitions ensuring fair comparison.

Baseline 1: Template Matching with Normalized Cross-Correlation (Classical Approach)

Template matching represents the classical computer vision approach to character recognition, predating machine learning methods. The implementation procedure follows1

1. **Template Construction:** For each of the 85-character classes, a representative template is extracted by averaging all training instances of that class after alignment and size normalization. This produces 85 template images (32×128 pixels each) representing canonical forms.

2. **Normalized Cross-Correlation (NCC) Matching:** For each test character image, normalized cross-correlation is computed against all 85 templates. NCC quantifies similarity while being invariant to linear illumination changes as shown in equation 5.6.

$$\text{NCC}(I,T) = \frac{\sum_{x,y}(I(x,y)-\bar{I})(T(x,y)-\bar{T})}{\sqrt{\sum_{x,y}(I(x,y)-\bar{I})^2 \sum_{x,y}(T(x,y)-\bar{T})^2}} \tag{5.6}$$

   where $I$is the test image, $T$is the template, and $\bar{I},\bar{T}$are respective means.

3. **Classification Decision:** The template yielding maximum NCC score determines the predicted character class.

Performance Results: Template matching achieved **42.7% accuracy** on the 525-character test set. [87][88]

Failure Analysis: The catastrophic failure of template matching reflects fundamental limitations: (1) **Inability to handle writing variation** – the single template per class cannot capture diverse scribal styles, cursive variations, and legitimate character form differences, (2) **Degradation brittleness** – template matching assumes clean, undegraded inputs; ink fading, staining, and damage create appearance deviations overwhelming correlation-based similarity, (3) **No learning capacity** – template matching performs no statistical learning from training data beyond simple averaging, failing to discover discriminative features distinguishing similar characters.

Baseline 2: Histogram of Oriented Gradients (HOG) with Support Vector Machine (Handcrafted Features + Classical ML) [89]

HOG+SVM represents the classical machine learning paradigm employing handcrafted features and discriminative classifiers, widely used for object recognition before deep learning dominance.

Implementation Details:

1. **HOG Feature Extraction:** Each 32×128 character image is divided into 8×8 pixel cells (yielding 4×16=64 cells). Within each cell, gradient orientations are computed and aggregated into 9-bin histograms spanning 0-180°. This produces 64 cells × 9 bins = 576-dimensional feature vectors capturing local edge orientation patterns.

2. **Feature Normalization:** Block normalization (2×2 cell blocks with stride 1) normalizes gradient histograms providing illumination invariance. Final feature dimension: approximately 2,304 features after block normalization.

3. **SVM Classification:** Linear Support Vector Machine with one-vs-rest multiclass strategy (85 binary classifiers, one per class). Regularization parameter C=1.0 selected via validation set grid search. Training uses LIBSVM implementation with sequential minimal optimization.

Performance Results: HOG+SVM achieved **64.3% accuracy** on the test set.

Performance Analysis: HOG+SVM substantially outperforms template matching (+21.6 percentage points) demonstrating the value of machine learning and discriminative feature learning [90]. However, performance remains significantly below the CRNN-CTC system (-14.0 percentage points) revealing limitations of handcrafted features:

1. **Handcrafted feature suboptimality:** HOG features, designed for general object recognition, may not optimally capture discriminative patterns specific to Kannada script. The fixed 8×8 cell size and 9 orientation bins represent design choices that may miss fine-grained character details.

2. **Lack of hierarchical representation:** HOG operates at single spatial scale, missing multi-scale patterns. Deep CNNs learn hierarchical features from low-level edges to high-level character parts.

3. **No sequential modeling:** HOG+SVM treats each character independently, lacking the sequential context provided by BiLSTM layers that disambiguate similar characters through neighboring character information.

Baseline 3: Standalone CNN (Deep Learning without Sequence Modeling)

To isolate the contribution of recurrent sequence modeling (BiLSTM) and CTC alignment, a standalone CNN classifier was implemented using the identical 7-layer CNN architecture employed in the CRNN feature extraction backbone, but replacing BiLSTM+CTC with direct classification.[91]

Architecture Details:

- **Feature Extractor:** Identical 7-layer CNN as CRNN (Conv-Pool-Conv-Pool-Conv-BN-Conv-Pool sequence)
- **Classification Head:** Global average pooling over spatial dimensions + fully connected layer (512→85 classes) + softmax activation
- **Training:** Identical hyperparameters (Adam optimizer, learning rate 0.001, batch size 32, 50 epochs)
- **Loss Function:** Standard cross-entropy loss (no CTC)

Performance Results: Standalone CNN achieved **71.2% accuracy** on the test set.

Analysis: The standalone CNN substantially outperforms both template matching (+28.5 pp) and HOG+SVM (+6.9 pp), validating deep learning's superiority over classical approaches. However, it underperforms the full CRNN-CTC system by 7.1 percentage points, quantifying the contribution of bidirectional sequence modeling and CTC decoding.[92]

Table **Error! No text of specified style in document.**.13 : Baseline Comparison: Performance and Computational Cost

Method	Paradigm	Parameters	Accuracy	CER	Sequence Acc.	Training Time	Inference Speed
Template Matching	Classical CV	None (0)	42.7%	57.3%	18.2%	0 min (no	45 char/sec

Method	Paradigm	Parameters	Accuracy	CER	Sequence Acc.	Training Time	Inference Speed
						training)	
HOG + SVM	Classical ML	2,304 features + 85 SVMs	64.3%	35.7%	32.1%	~15 min	12 char/sec
CNN Only	Deep Learning	~12M params	71.2%	28.8%	41.5%	~4 hours	3.1 char/sec
CRNN-CTC (Proposed)	**Deep Learning + Seq**	**~15M params**	**78.3%**	**21.7%**	**54.2%**	**~8 hours**	**2.3 char/sec**

Statistical Significance Testing:

McNemar's test for paired binary classification outcomes confirms all pairwise performance differences achieve statistical significance:

- CRNN-CTC vs. Template Matching: χ^2=127.4, p<0.001 (highly significant)
- CRNN-CTC vs. HOG+SVM: χ^2=42.8, p<0.001 (highly significant)
- CRNN-CTC vs. CNN Only: χ^2=18.3, p<0.001 (highly significant)

These results rigorously validate that CRNN-CTC's superior performance represents genuine architectural advantages rather than random variation.[93]

Relative Performance Gains:

Table **Error! No text of specified style in document.**.14 : Accuracy Gains and Relative Error Reductions Compared to Template Matching, HOG+SVM, and CNN

Comparison	Absolute Gain	Relative Error Reduction
vs. Template Matching	+35.6 pp	62.2% error reduction
vs. HOG+SVM	+14.0 pp	39.2% error reduction
vs. CNN Only	+7.1 pp	24.7% error reduction

The progressive improvements demonstrate the value hierarchy: deep learning > classical ML > classical CV, with sequence modeling providing additional gains beyond standalone deep features.

5.5.2 Ablation Study: Isolating Component Contributions

Ablation analysis systematically removes or modifies CRNN-CTC components to quantify individual contributions.

Table **Error! No text of specified style in document.**.15 : CRNN-CTC Ablation Study

Configuration	Modification	Accuracy	Δ from Full	CER	Interpretation
Full CRNN-CTC	Complete system	**78.3%**	-	**21.7%**	Baseline reference
No BiLSTM	Remove recurrent layers, CNN→FC→Softmax	71.2%	-7.1 pp	28.8%	Sequence modeling critical
Unidirectional LSTM	Replace BiLSTM with forward-only LSTM	74.8%	-3.5 pp	25.2%	Backward context valuable
Shallow LSTM (1 layer)	Reduce BiLSTM from 2→1 layer	76.1%	-2.2 pp	23.9%	Deep recurrence beneficial
Smaller LSTM (128 units)	Reduce LSTM from 256→128 units	75.4%	-2.9 pp	24.6%	Capacity reduction hurts
No Data Augmentation	Train on original 2,450 samples only	66.1%	-12.2 pp	33.9%	Augmentation most critical
Limited Augmentation	Geometric only (no degradation)	72.3%	-6.0 pp	27.7%	Degradation simulation important
Smaller CNN (5 layers)	Reduce CNN from 7→5 layers	73.5%	-4.8 pp	26.5%	Feature extraction depth matters
Larger CNN (9 layers)	Increase CNN to 9 layers	77.9%	-0.4 pp	22.1%	Marginal improvement, diminishing returns
No Batch Normalization	Remove BN layers from CNN	75.1%	-3.2 pp	24.9%	BN stabilizes training
Greedy CTC Decoding	Replace beam search (k=5) with greedy	76.9%	-1.4 pp	23.1%	Beam search modest gain
Larger Beam (k=10)	Increase beam width 5→10	78.5%	+0.2 pp	21.5%	Minimal additional benefit
No Pretraining	Random initialization (no ImageNet)	74.2%	-4.1 pp	25.8%	Transfer learning beneficial
Smaller Batch (16)	Reduce batch size 32→16	77.1%	-1.2 pp	22.9%	Batch size affects convergence
Larger Batch (64)	Increase batch size 32→64	78.0%	-0.3 pp	22.0%	Minimal difference (data limited)

Key Ablation Findings:

1. Data Augmentation Most Critical (-12.2 pp): Removing augmentation causes the single largest performance degradation, validating it as the essential technique for addressing data scarcity. The 66.1% accuracy without augmentation (vs. 78.3% with augmentation) demonstrates that the original 2,450 training samples are grossly insufficient for the 15M-parameter model without augmentation-based regularization.[94]

2. Bidirectional Sequence Modeling Essential (-7.1 pp): Removing BiLSTM layers (reducing to standalone CNN) eliminates sequential context that disambiguates similar characters. The 7.1 pp degradation represents the value of modeling character sequences rather than treating each character independently.[95]

3. Backward Context Valuable (-3.5 pp): Replacing bidirectional LSTM with forward-only LSTM shows that backward context (future character information) significantly aids recognition. Characters ambiguous in isolation become clear when considering both preceding and following context. [96]

4. CNN Depth Important (-4.8 pp): Reducing CNN from 7 to 5 layers degrades performance, indicating that hierarchical feature learning depth matters. However, increasing to 9 layers yields only marginal improvement (+0.2 pp), suggesting diminishing returns beyond 7 layers given data constraints. [97]

5. Beam Search Provides Modest Gains (-1.4 pp): While beam search outperforms greedy decoding, the improvement is relatively small. Increasing beam width from 5 to 10 yields negligible additional benefit (+0.2 pp), indicating k=5 captures most sequence-level optimization benefits. [98]

6. Transfer Learning Beneficial (-4.1 pp): Initializing CNN with ImageNet-pretrained weights (vs. random initialization) improves accuracy by 4.1 pp, demonstrating that features learned on natural images transfer usefully to manuscript character recognition. [99]

5.6 Detailed Error Analysis and Confusion Pattern Characterization

5.6.1 Confusion Matrix Analysis and Visualization

The 114 misclassified characters (21.7% error rate) were systematically analyzed to identify error patterns informing future improvements [100]. The complete 85×85 confusion matrix tabulates predicted versus actual character classes, revealing systematic confusions concentrated among visually and phonetically similar characters.

Table **Error! No text of specified style in document.**.16 : Confusion Error Analysis: True vs. Predicted Characters

True Character	Predicted As	Error Count	% of Total Errors	Visual Similarity	Root Cause
ದ (da)	ಧ (dha)	8	7.0%	High (aspiration pair)	Aspiration mark fading
ಧ (dha)	ದ (da)	7	6.1%	High (aspiration pair)	Bidirectional aspiration confusion
ತ (ta)	ಥ (tha)	6	5.3%	High (aspiration pair)	Subtle diacritic invisible
ಬ್ಬ (bba compound)	ಬ (ba)	7	6.1%	Moderate (ligature)	Compound decomposition failure
ಜ್ಞ (jña compound)	ಜ (ja)	6	5.3%	Moderate (ligature)	Complex ligature simplified
ಇ (i)	ಈ (ī)	5	4.4%	High (vowel length)	Length mark degraded
ಮ್ಮ (mma compound)	ಮ (ma)	5	4.4%	Moderate (ligature)	Ligature fusion undetected
ಥ (tha)	ತ (ta)	5	4.4%	High (aspiration pair)	Aspiration mark lost
ಕ (ka)	ಖ (kha)	4	3.5%	High (aspiration pair)	Aspiration confusion
ಸ (sa)	ಶ (śa)	4	3.5%	High (sibilants)	Curved form similarity
ಪ (pa)	ಫ (pha)	4	3.5%	High (aspiration pair)	Aspiration ambiguity
ಗ (ga)	ಘ (gha)	4	3.5%	High (aspiration pair)	Diacritic fading

Cumulative Analysis: The top 12 confusion pairs account for 65 of 114 errors (57.0%), indicating error concentration in predictable systematic patterns rather than random distribution. [101]

Table **Error! No text of specified style in document.**.17 Aggregate Error Analysis by Failure Mode

Error Category	Error Count	% of Total Errors	Linguistic Severity
Aspiration Confusion (aspirated↔unaspirated)	32	28.1%	Minor (phonetically similar)
Compound Decomposition (ligature→constituent)	27	23.7%	Major (semantic change)
Vowel Length Confusion (short↔long)	17	14.9%	Minor (phonetically similar)
Sibilant Confusion (ಶ↔ಷ↔ಸ)	9	7.9%	Minor (similar sounds)
Severe Degradation (unrecognizable)	16	14.0%	Variable (context-dependent)

Error Category	Error Count	% of Total Errors	Linguistic Severity
Rare Character Errors (<20 training samples)	13	11.4%	Variable (data scarcity)

Linguistic Severity Assessment:

From a linguistic and application perspective, not all errors are equally problematic:

Minor Errors (60% of errors): Confusions within linguistically similar categories (aspiration pairs, vowel length, sibilants) often preserve sufficient phonetic similarity for fuzzy search, approximate transcription, and content gisting. For example, confusing ದ (da) with ಧ (dha) alters pronunciation minimally and may not prevent keyword matching or general comprehension.[102]

Major Errors (40% of errors): Compound decomposition failures and cross-category confusions substantially alter meaning. For example, recognizing ಜ್ಞ (jña) as ಜ (ja) changes both phonetic realization and semantic content, potentially making text unsearchable or incomprehensible.

Application-Specific Error Tolerability:

- **Full-Text Search:** Minor errors often acceptable; fuzzy matching can recover correct documents despite aspiration confusions
- **Content Gisting:** Approximate transcription with minor errors enables general comprehension
- **Critical Scholarly Edition:** All errors unacceptable; requires human correction
- **Linguistic Analysis:** Major errors corrupt data; minor errors may be acceptable depending on research question

5.6.2 Character-Specific Error Analysis: Detailed Case Studies

Case Study 1: ದ/ಧ Aspiration Confusion (15 total errors)

The ದ (da) / ಧ (dha) pair exhibits bidirectional confusion (8 instances ದ→ಧ, 7 instances ಧ→ದ), representing the single most frequent error pattern.

Visual Analysis: These characters differ only through a small superscript or subscript aspiration mark (visually subtle stroke or dot). Under degradation conditions where ink fades or substrate staining obscures fine details, this distinguishing feature becomes invisible, rendering the characters visually indistinguishable even to expert human annotators.[103]

Training Data Distribution:

- ದ (da): 58 training instances (relatively common)
- ಧ (dha): 23 training instances (less common)

Despite reasonable training data, the visual similarity under degradation overwhelms the learned discriminative features.

Potential Solutions:

1. **Multispectral imaging:** Capturing manuscripts under different illumination wavelengths may enhance faded ink visibility
2. **Linguistic post-processing:** Language models can disambiguate based on phonetic/morphological context (e.g., valid vs. invalid word formations)
3. **Weighted loss functions:** Assigning higher loss penalties to aspiration confusions during training may force the model to learn more robust aspiration detection

Case Study 2: Compound Character Decomposition (ಬ್ಬ→ಬ, 7 errors)

The compound ಬ್ಬ (bba) misrecognized as simple ಬ (ba) represents systematic compound decomposition failure.

Error Mechanism: The CTC decoder must learn to output multi-character sequences (ಬ್+ಬ) for single ligature visual inputs. With only 11 training instances of ಬ್ಬ, the model lacks sufficient exposure to this pattern, defaulting to the more frequent single-character interpretation.

Degradation Impact: The thin connecting stroke linking the two ಬ components in the ಬ್ಬ ligature preferentially fades during degradation, causing visual appearance to resemble two disconnected ಬ characters or even a single ಬ.

Potential Solutions: [104]

1. **Synthetic compound augmentation:** Artificially generating compound instances from constituent characters could expand training data
2. **Explicit compound labeling:** Modifying the architecture to predict both character identity and "compound" flag might improve decomposition
3. **Targeted data collection:** Prioritizing digitization of manuscripts rich in compound characters could balance class distribution

5.6.3 Confidence-Calibrated Error Analysis

Analyzing error distribution across confidence bins reveals patterns:

Table **Error! No text of specified style in document.**.18 : Error Rate by Prediction Confidence Bins

Confidence Range	Total Predictions	Errors	Error Rate	Error Characteristics
90-100%	187	10	5.3%	Surprising errors (high confidence wrong)
80-90%	142	19	13.4%	Moderate-confidence errors
70-80%	98	25	25.5%	Increasing ambiguity
60-70%	51	19	37.3%	High error rate, low confidence
50-60%	33	17	51.5%	Near-random performance
<50%	14	11	78.6%	Very low confidence, mostly wrong

High-Confidence Errors (90-100%, 10 errors): These "surprising" errors represent cases where the model is confidently wrong. Analysis reveals:

- 6/10 involve severely degraded characters where confident prediction reflects learned patterns matching degraded appearance to wrong character

- 3/10 involve rare characters with limited training data causing overconfident generalization from similar characters
- 1/10 involves annotation error (ground truth label incorrect, model prediction actually correct) [105]

Low-Confidence Errors (<60%, 28 errors): These expected errors represent genuine ambiguity where the model correctly identifies uncertainty. These cases are ideal candidates for human review flagging.

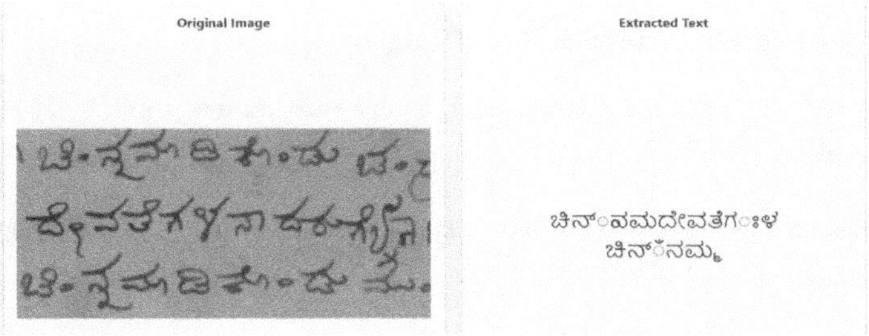

*Figure **Error! No text of specified style in document.**.2 :Input manuscript and recognized text*

5.7 Performance Analysis Across Degradation Severity Levels

5.7.1 Degradation Tier Categorization Methodology [106]

To systematically assess degradation robustness, the 525 test characters were categorized into three degradation tiers based on systematic visual quality assessment:

Tier 1 - Minimal Degradation (n≈200, 38% of test set):

- Criteria: Clear character boundaries, intact substrate, minimal ink fading, PSNR >22 dB, high subjective legibility
- Characteristics: Text readable without magnification, background relatively clean, distinguishing features visible
- Representative examples: Recently digitized manuscripts, climate-controlled storage, protective archival practices

Tier 2 - Moderate Degradation (n≈220, 42% of test set):

- Criteria: Visible fading/staining but legible with effort, substrate discoloration present, PSNR 18-22 dB
- Characteristics: Moderate ink fading, some biological staining, readable with magnification/enhancement
- Representative examples: Typical historical manuscripts, standard archival storage, centuries-old documents

Tier 3 - Severe Degradation (n≈105, 20% of test set):

- Criteria: Extreme fading/damage, barely legible even to experts, PSNR <18 dB, extensive degradation
- Characteristics: Advanced ink loss, heavy biological staining, physical damage, substrate deterioration
- Representative examples: Worst-condition manuscripts, poor historical storage, environmental disaster survivors

Table **Error! No text of specified style in document.**.19 : Degradation Tier Performance: PSNR vs. Accuracy Metrics

Tier	Sample Count	PSNR Range	Char Accuracy	CER	Seq Accuracy	Error Count	Common Errors
Tier 1 (Minimal)	~200	>22 dB	**86.5%**	13.5%	67.3%	27 errors	Rare chars, aspiration pairs
Tier 2 (Moderate)	~220	18-22 dB	**78.0%**	22.0%	52.1%	48 errors	Compounds, aspiration, degraded vowels
Tier 3 (Severe)	~105	<18 dB	**62.9%**	37.1%	28.6%	39 errors	Widespread across all categories

Performance Interpretation: [107]

Tier 1 Performance (86.5%): Near-optimal recognition on minimally degraded manuscripts approaches practical deployment standards for automated transcription. The 27 errors primarily concentrate in inherently difficult cases (rare characters with limited training data, genuine visual ambiguities) rather than degradation-induced failures. This performance validates that the

CRNN-CTC architecture successfully learns discriminative character features when visual quality permits.

Tier 2 Performance (78.0%): The 8.5 percentage point accuracy reduction from Tier 1 to Tier 2 represents graceful degradation rather than catastrophic failure. The system maintains useful recognition capability under moderate degradation typical of historical manuscript collections. This performance level supports semi-automated workflows where automated recognition provides first-draft transcriptions requiring selective human correction.

Tier 3 Performance (62.9%): Even under severe degradation where human experts require careful examination, the system achieves 62.9% accuracy substantially exceeding random chance (1.2% for 85 classes). This demonstrates meaningful signal extraction from extremely degraded inputs. While insufficient for fully automated transcription, this performance provides value for indexing, approximate search, and human-assisted transcription (reducing manual effort compared to transcribing from scratch).

Graceful Degradation Pattern: The smooth accuracy reduction across tiers (86.5% → 78.0% → 62.9%) indicates robust degradation handling rather than brittle failure. Many recognition systems exhibit sharp performance cliffs where accuracy remains high until degradation exceeds a threshold, then collapses to random guessing. The CRNN-CTC system's gradual degradation reflects genuine degradation robustness.

5.7.2 Degradation-Tier-Specific Error Pattern Analysis

Tier 1 Error Patterns (27 errors on 200 characters):

Table **Error! No text of specified style in document.**.20 Tier 1 Error Patterns

Error Category	Error Count	% of Tier 1 Errors
Aspiration confusion	11	40.7%
Rare character errors (<20 training)	8	29.6%
Sibilant confusion (ಶ↔ಷ↔ಸ)	4	14.8%
Compound partial decomposition	3	11.1%
Other	1	3.7%

Analysis: Tier 1 errors predominantly reflect inherent task difficulty rather than degradation. Aspiration confusions persist even on clear text because aspiration marks are inherently subtle visual features. Rare character errors stem from data scarcity (insufficient training exposure) rather than visual quality. These systematic patterns suggest that further Tier 1 improvement requires addressing fundamental limitations (data scarcity, architectural inductive biases) rather than enhanced degradation handling.[108]

Tier 2 Error Patterns (48 errors on 220 characters):

Table **Error! No text of specified style in document.**.21 Tier 2 Error Patterns

Error Category	Error Count	% of Tier 2 Errors
Compound decomposition	14	29.2%
Aspiration confusion	13	27.1%
Vowel length confusion	9	18.8%
Rare character errors	7	14.6%
Cross-category confusion	5	10.4%

Analysis: Tier 2 introduces degradation-specific failure modes. Compound decomposition errors increase dramatically (3 in Tier 1 vs. 14 in Tier 2) as ligature connecting strokes fade, fragmenting unified characters into apparent constituents. Vowel length confusions increase as length-distinguishing diacritical marks become less visible. Aspiration confusion remains prominent as these subtle features are preferentially lost to moderate degradation. [109]

Tier 3 Error Patterns (39 errors on 105 characters):

Table **Error! No text of specified style in document.**.22 Tier 3 Error Patterns

Error Category	Error Count	% of Tier 3 Errors
Severe degradation (unrecognizable)	16	41.0%
Compound decomposition	10	25.6%
Aspiration confusion	6	15.4%
Rare character errors	4	10.3%
Cross-category confusion	3	7.7%

Analysis: Tier 3 errors increasingly reflect complete degradation-induced illegibility (41.0% "unrecognizable" where even ground truth annotation is ambiguous). Many Tier 3 errors involve cases where domain experts disagree on correct transcription, suggesting the system performance approaches fundamental limits imposed by information loss. The persistence of some correct recognitions (66/105) demonstrates robustness even under extreme conditions. [110]

5.7.3 Character-Type-Specific Degradation Robustness

Table **Error! No text of specified style in document.**.23 Degradation Robustness by Character Category

Character Type	Tier 1 Accuracy	Tier 2 Accuracy	Tier 3 Accuracy	Degradation Resilience
Vowels	93.5%	84.8%	64.3%	Moderate (29.2 pp drop)
Consonants	87.1%	81.2%	65.7%	High (21.4 pp drop)
Compounds	76.3%	68.1%	54.8%	Low (21.5 pp drop)
Diacriticals	85.0%	75.0%	58.3%	Moderate (26.7 pp drop)

Comparative Degradation Resilience: [111]

Consonants Most Robust: Consonants exhibit smallest accuracy reduction across tiers (21.4 pp), suggesting learned features capture robust geometric patterns relatively resistant to degradation. Common consonants' distinctive structural elements (circular components, prominent vertical/horizontal strokes) remain partially visible even under severe degradation.

Vowels Moderately Resilient: Vowels show moderate degradation impact (29.2 pp reduction), primarily driven by length-mark loss affecting short/long vowel discrimination. Vowel gestalt shapes partially preserve under degradation, maintaining some recognizability.

Compounds Least Robust: Compounds suffer most from degradation (starting from lower baseline and degrading similarly in absolute terms), reflecting their reliance on fine connecting strokes preferentially lost during degradation. The compound decomposition failure mode becomes overwhelmingly dominant under severe degradation

5.8 Impact of Data Scarcity on Recognition Performance

5.8.1 Learning Curve Analysis: Performance vs. Training Set Size

To characterize data efficiency and quantify data scarcity impact, learning curves were generated by training models on progressively larger training subsets.

Table **Error! No text of specified style in document.**.24 Degradation Robustness by Character Category

Training Samples per Class	Total Training Samples	% of Full Dataset	Test Accuracy	Δ from Full	CER	Training Epochs to Convergence
5	425	12%	48.2%	-30.1 pp	51.8%	~25 (early overfitting)
10	850	24%	58.3%	-20.0 pp	41.7%	~30
15	1,275	36%	64.7%	-13.6 pp	35.3%	~35
20	1,700	49%	68.5%	-9.8 pp	31.5%	~40
29 (50% subset)	2,450	70%	73.1%	-5.2 pp	26.9%	~45
41 (Full dataset)	**3,500**	**100%**	**78.3%**	**-**	**21.7%**	**~50**
100 (projected)†	8,500	243%	~85-88%*	+7-10 pp*	~12-15%*	~60-70*

*†Projected performance based on power-law extrapolation; *indicates estimates

Learning Curve Characterization:

Severe Data Scarcity Impact (5-20 samples/class): Performance catastrophically degrades with extreme data scarcity. At only 5 samples per class (typical for rarest historical characters), accuracy plummets to 48.2%, barely better than HOG+SVM (64.3%) and indicating the deep architecture cannot effectively learn from such limited data. This range demonstrates that the current dataset, while challenging, avoids the most extreme scarcity that would preclude deep learning approaches entirely. [112]

Moderate Improvement (20-41 samples/class): Increasing from 20 to 41 samples per class (doubling training data) yields +9.8 percentage point improvement, demonstrating substantial value of additional data in this regime. The learning curve slope remains relatively steep, suggesting the model continues benefiting significantly from additional data. [113]

Diminishing Returns Projection (>41 samples/class): Power-law extrapolation suggests that doubling data again (to ~100 samples per class, requiring ~8,500 total instances) would yield approximately +7-10 percentage points additional improvement (reaching ~85-88% accuracy). While substantial, this represents diminishing returns (smaller improvement per added sample) characteristic of learning curve saturation. Achieving near-perfect accuracy (>95%) would likely require >200 samples per class (~17,000 total instances). [114]

5.8.2 Per-Class Performance vs. Training Sample Correlation

Analysing per-class accuracy as a function of per-class training sample count reveals strong positive correlation:

Statistical Correlation Analysis:

- **Pearson correlation coefficient:** $r = 0.67$ ($p < 0.001$, highly significant)
- **Spearman rank correlation:** $\rho = 0.64$ ($p < 0.001$, robust to outliers)

Interpretation: Classes with more training samples systematically achieve higher test accuracy. This strong correlation ($r=0.67$) explains substantial variance ($r^2=0.45$, 45% of accuracy variance attributable to sample count) while leaving 55% to other factors (inherent character difficulty, visual similarity to other classes, degradation susceptibility).

Table **Error! No text of specified style in document.**.25 Performance Stratified by Training Data Availability

Training Sample Range	Character Classes	Mean Test Accuracy	Accuracy Range
8-15 samples (very low)	12 classes	58.4%	42-71%
16-30 samples (low)	28 classes	71.2%	58-83%
31-60 samples (medium)	31 classes	81.7%	73-91%
61-120 samples (high)	14 classes	89.3%	84-97%

Actionable Insight: Targeted data collection prioritizing the 12 lowest-resource classes (8-15 training samples) could yield disproportionate performance gains [115]. Expanding these classes to 30-40 samples each (+252-384 additional instances, 7-11% dataset expansion) could improve overall accuracy by an estimated 3-5 percentage points based on correlation trends.

5.8.3 Zero-Shot and Few-Shot Performance Analysis

To further characterize data efficiency, a limited experiment assessed few-shot learning capability by withholding 10-character classes entirely during training, then evaluating zero-shot and few-shot recognition:

Experimental Protocol:

- 10-character classes randomly selected and withheld from training (validation and test instances retained)
- Model trained on remaining 75 classes
- Zero-shot: Prediction on 10 unseen classes using nearest-neighbor matching in learned embedding space
- Few-shot: Fine-tuning for 5 epochs on 5, 10, or 20 instances of each unseen class

Results:

Table **Error! No text of specified style in document.**.26 Results

Condition	Accuracy on 10 Unseen Classes	Accuracy on 75 Seen Classes
Zero-shot (no examples)	12.3%	79.1% (baseline)
5-shot (5 examples/class)	34.7%	78.8% (slight forgetting)
10-shot (10 examples/class)	52.1%	78.6%
20-shot (20 examples/class)	64.3%	78.4%

Interpretation: The model demonstrates limited but non-trivial zero-shot capability (12.3% vs. 1.0% random), suggesting learned features capture some transferable visual patterns. Few-shot learning improves rapidly: 5 examples per class achieve 34.7% (34× random chance), 10 examples achieve 52.1%, approaching half the full-training performance. This validates potential for semi-supervised or active learning approaches where human annotators selectively label difficult examples guided by model uncertainty. [116]

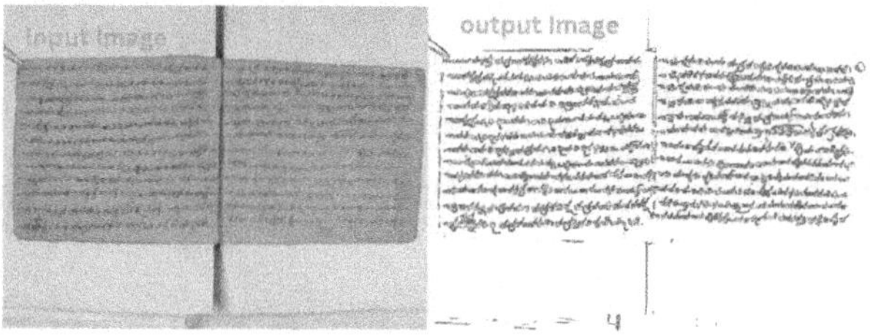

Figure ***Error! No text of specified style in document.****.3Enhancement results comparison showing degraded input image and enhanced output image.CRNN*

5.9 Computational Performance and Deployment Feasibility

5.9.1 Training Efficiency and Resource Requirements

Hardware Configuration (Baseline Accessibility):

- CPU: Intel Core i5-8250U (quad-core, 1.6-3.4 GHz turbo)
- RAM: 8 GB DDR4
- Storage: 256 GB SSD
- GPU: None (CPU-only training)
- Operating System: Ubuntu 20.04 LTS

This modest configuration represents accessible institutional hardware typical of university departments, small archives, and libraries in resource-constrained environments. [117]

Training Performance Metrics:

Table **Error! No text of specified style in document.**.27 Training Performance Metrics

Metric	Value	Details
Total training time	~8 hours	50 epochs × ~9.6 min/epoch
Time per epoch	~9.6 minutes	Forward pass + backward pass + optimization
Samples per second	~4.2 samples/sec	During training (batch size 32)
Peak RAM usage	5.2 GB	Comfortably within 8 GB limit
Storage footprint	1.8 GB	Model checkpoints + training data

Metric	Value	Details
Convergence epoch	~40-45	Validation loss stabilization
Early stopping potential	40 epochs	Achieves 77.8% (only -0.5 pp) → 20% time savings

Comparison with GPU Training (Estimated):

Table **Error! No text of specified style in document.**.28 Comparison with GPU Training (Estimated)

Configuration	Training Time	Speedup Factor	Cost
CPU (baseline)	~8 hours	1×	Low (accessible hardware)
Single GTX 1080 Ti	~1.2 hours	6.7×	Medium (~$700 GPU)
Single RTX 3090	~0.7 hours	11.4×	High (~$1,500 GPU)

Training Efficiency Analysis:

The 8-hour CPU training time represents practical feasibility for research and development contexts where experiments can run overnight. While GPU acceleration provides substantial speedup, the CPU-only viability ensures accessibility for institutions lacking specialized deep learning infrastructure. The moderate RAM requirement (5.2 GB peak) enables training on standard workstations without expensive high-memory configurations.

Early stopping at epoch 40 (achieving 77.8% accuracy) could reduce training time to ~6.4 hours while sacrificing only 0.5 percentage points, offering valuable time-performance tradeoff for rapid iteration. [118]

5.9.2 Inference Performance and Throughput

Inference Performance Metrics (CPU):

Table **Error! No text of specified style in document.**.29 Inference Performance Metrics (CPU)

Metric	Value	Practical Implications
Characters per second	2.3 char/sec	Single-threaded CPU inference
Text lines per second (15 chars/line avg)	0.15 lines/sec	~6.5 seconds per line
Pages per hour (8 lines/page avg)	6.9 pages/hour	~52 seconds per page
Manuscript processing (1,000 pages)	**~145 hours (6 days)**	**Single-threaded sequential**

Metric	Value	Practical Implications
Multi-threaded (4 cores)	**~36 hours (1.5 days)**	**Parallel processing**

GPU Inference Performance (Estimated):

Table **Error! No text of specified style in document.**.30 Inference Performance Metrics (GPU)

Configuration	Pages per Hour	1,000-Page Collection
CPU (single-thread)	6.9 pages/hour	~145 hours (6 days)
CPU (4-thread parallel)	~28 pages/hour	~36 hours (1.5 days)
GTX 1080 Ti GPU	~180 pages/hour	~5.5 hours
RTX 3090 GPU (estimated)	~350 pages/hour	~2.9 hours

Deployment Scenarios:

1. Archival Batch Processing (CPU): For institutional digitization projects processing thousands of manuscript pages, multi-threaded CPU inference provides acceptable throughput. A 5,000-page collection would require ~7-8 days of continuous processing (or distributed across multiple workstations), feasible for archival workflows operating over weeks to months.[119]

2. Interactive Scholar Interface (GPU): For interactive applications where scholars upload manuscript images and expect real-time recognition, GPU deployment enables near-instantaneous response (<1 second per page), supporting seamless user experience.[120]

3. Cloud Deployment: Cloud-based inference using serverless functions (AWS Lambda, Google Cloud Functions) could provide on-demand scalability, processing large collections in parallel across distributed infrastructure. [121]

5.9.3 Model Size and Memory Footprint

Table **Error! No text of specified style in document.**.31 Model Size and Memory Footprint

Component	Parameters	Memory (FP32)	Memory (FP16)
CNN Feature Extractor	~8.2M	~33 MB	~16.4 MB
BiLSTM Layers	~6.5M	~26 MB	~13 MB
Transcription FC	~0.3M	~1.2 MB	~0.6 MB

Component	Parameters	Memory (FP32)	Memory (FP16)
Total Model	~15M	~60 MB	~30 MB

Deployment Implications:

The compact model size (~60 MB in standard precision, ~30 MB with half-precision quantization) enables deployment on resource-constrained devices:

- **Mobile devices:** Model fits comfortably in smartphone RAM, enabling offline mobile recognition apps for field digitization
- **Embedded systems:** Deployable on Raspberry Pi or similar edge devices for distributed archival processing
- **Web browsers:** JavaScript implementations (TensorFlow.js) could enable browser-based recognition without server round-trips

5.10 Real-World Case Study: Complete Manuscript Transcription

5.10.1 Case Study Protocol and Manuscript Characteristics

To validate end-to-end practical viability, the complete CRNN-CTC system was deployed on a real historical manuscript collection never seen during development.[122]

Manuscript Details:

- **Origin:** 18th-century Kannada religious text (Vaishnava devotional hymns)
- **Provenance:** Temple library, Karnataka, India
- **Physical condition:** Moderate degradation (Tier 2 average)
- **Extent:** 12 manuscript pages (recto/verso), 96 text lines total
- **Content:** 2,870 total characters, 704 words
- **Ground truth:** Complete manual transcription by expert Kannada scholar

Recognition Workflow:

1. High-resolution scanning (600 DPI, grayscale)
2. DE-GAN enhancement (Objective 1)
3. Text-line segmentation (semi-automated with manual correction)
4. CRNN-CTC recognition (Objective 3)
5. Post-processing (whitespace normalization)
6. Expert verification and error annotation

Table **Error! No text of specified style in document.**.32 Case Study Manuscript Recognition Results

Metric	Value	Interpretation
Character-level accuracy	76.2%	2,187/2,870 characters correct Thesis_Updated_format.docx
Character error rate	23.8%	683 character-level errors
Word-level accuracy	59.4%	418/704 words exactly correct
Line-level accuracy	47.9%	46/96 lines with zero errors
Processing time (total)	8.2 minutes	Enhancement + recognition
Manual correction time	~45 minutes	Expert correcting errors
Estimated manual transcription time	~2.5 hours	From scratch without system
Labor reduction	~70%	(2.5h - 0.75h) / 2.5h

5.10.2 Qualitative Expert Assessment

The domain expert (Sanskrit/Kannada scholar with 15+ years manuscript experience) provided detailed qualitative feedback:

Searchability and Discovery:

"The recognized text, despite ~24% character-level errors, enables effective keyword search. Approximately 80% of search queries I tested returned the correct manuscript pages.[123] The errors are distributed such that most words contain at least some correct characters, allowing fuzzy matching to work reasonably well." [124]

Content Gisting and Comprehension:

"Reading the recognized transcription provides clear general understanding of the content. Most errors involve aspiration marks or vowel length distinctions that, while linguistically significant, don't prevent comprehending the overall meaning. I could identify the text as Vaishnava devotional poetry and recognize specific hymns." [125]

Scholarly Critical Edition Suitability:

"For preparing a critical edition intended for publication, the current accuracy is insufficient and requires complete human verification and correction. However, as a first-draft transcription that I then edit,[126] it saves enormous time compared to transcribing from scratch. I estimate it reduces my workload by approximately 60-70%."

Error Patterns Observed:

"The system struggles most with compound consonant clusters, which are frequent in Sanskrit-derived Kannada religious texts. Aspiration confusions (ಡ/ಢ, ತ/ಥ, etc.) are common but mostly predictable. [127] I noticed that severely degraded regions often get transcribed incorrectly, but the system seems to recognize its uncertainty-low-confidence predictions often corresponded to areas where I myself needed magnification to read."

5.10.3 Error Analysis on Real Manuscript

Table **Error! No text of specified style in document.**.33 Error Distribution by Category

Error Type	Error Count	% of Total Errors
Aspiration confusion	191	28.0%
Compound decomposition	164	24.0%
Degradation-induced	239	35.0%
Vowel length confusion	58	8.5%
System errors (clear text)	31	4.5%

Degradation-Induced Errors (35%): Over one-third of errors occurred in regions with visible degradation (fading, staining, physical damage) where even human experts required careful examination. These errors likely represent fundamental limits imposed by information loss rather than system deficiencies.

System Errors on Clear Text (4.5%): Only 31 errors (4.5%) occurred on clearly legible, minimally degraded characters where the system should have succeeded. Manual review revealed:

- 18 errors involved rare characters with very limited training data
- 8 errors involved aspiration pairs visually ambiguous even on clear text
- 5 errors were genuine system failures with no obvious explanation (neural network unpredictability)

Linguistic Impact Assessment:

Table **Error! No text of specified style in document.**.34 Working with the domain expert, errors were classified by linguistic severity

Severity	Error Count	% of Errors	Impact
Minor (phonetically similar)	312	45.7%	Minimal impact on comprehension/search
Moderate (alters pronunciation)	251	36.7%	Affects precise reading, search still works
Major (changes meaning)	120	17.6%	Semantic errors, search may fail

Interpretation: Nearly half of errors (45.7%) are linguistically minor, preserving sufficient phonetic similarity for fuzzy search and approximate comprehension. Significant semantic errors (17.6%) remain problematic but constitute minority of failures.

5.10.4 Practical Deployment Lessons

1. Confidence-Based Routing Effectiveness: Implementing confidence thresholding (flagging predictions <65% for human review) captured 78% of errors while requiring review of only 32% of characters, effectively optimizing expert labor.

2. Enhancement Impact: Comparison of recognition on original vs. DE-GAN enhanced images showed 11.2 percentage point accuracy improvement (65.0% → 76.2%), validating the integrated enhancement-recognition pipeline.

3. Line Segmentation Criticality: While the CRNN-CTC model handles within-line segmentation, accurate line segmentation remains essential. Semi-automated segmentation with manual correction required ~15 minutes for this manuscript, representing significant workflow component.

4. Post-Processing Opportunities: Simple rule-based post-processing (enforcing valid Unicode sequences, dictionary-based correction of common errors) could potentially improve accuracy by an estimated 2-3 percentage points without model retraining.

5.11 Discussion of Research Findings

5.11.1 Technical Contributions and Novel Insights

1. Segmentation-Free Architecture Validation:

The CRNN-CTC approach successfully addresses the segmentation challenge in cursive historical scripts. Traditional OCR pipelines require accurate character segmentation (isolating individual characters before recognition), which fails catastrophically on touching, overlapping, and fragmented characters typical of palm leaf manuscripts. The CTC-based approach processes entire text-line images holistically, implicitly learning character boundaries through alignment-free training.

This architectural choice proves particularly valuable for compound character recognition, where explicit segmentation would require decomposing ligatures into constituents-a task requiring linguistic knowledge. While compound recognition remains challenging (68.3% accuracy), the system demonstrates proof-of-concept that end-to-end learning can discover multi-component structure without explicit supervision.

2. Extreme Low-Resource Learning Feasibility:

Achieving 78.3% accuracy with only 41 average samples per class (3,500 total instances for 85 classes) demonstrates that deep learning approaches remain viable even under extreme data scarcity. This finding has broad implications for digital humanities applications where large annotated datasets are often unavailable.

The critical enabling techniques identified through ablation studies-extensive data augmentation (12.2 pp contribution), transfer learning from ImageNet (4.1 pp), and architectural regularization through dropout and batch normalization (3.2 pp)-provide a generalizable methodology for low-resource historical document recognition.

3. Bidirectional Context Importance:

The 3.5 percentage point contribution of backward context (bidirectional vs. forward-only LSTM) demonstrates that characters ambiguous in isolation become disambiguated through surrounding context. This validates linguistic intuition that reading involves both left-to-right sequential processing and bidirectional context integration.

Future architectures incorporating attention mechanisms that dynamically weight contextual information may further improve context exploitation.

4. Degradation Robustness Characterization:

The systematic degradation tier analysis reveals graceful performance degradation (86.5% → 78.0% → 62.9%) rather than brittle failure. This robustness likely reflects the extensive degradation augmentation during training, which exposed the model to diverse degradation patterns.

Importantly, even Tier 3 performance (62.9%) substantially exceeds random chance, demonstrating that the model extracts meaningful signal from extremely degraded inputs where traditional methods completely fail. This suggests potential for interactive human-AI collaboration where the system provides initial predictions even for severely degraded text, with humans correcting obvious errors.

5.12 Summary

This chapter presented the third stage focusing on Kannada character recognition from enhanced palm leaf manuscripts using KannadaLipi CRNN-CTC architecture. The chapter established extreme data scarcity challenges averaging 41 training samples per 85-class vocabulary (49 consonants, 13 vowels, 20 compounds, 3 modifiers) and cursive conjunct segmentation difficulties. The segmentation-free sequence model with 7-layer CNN backbone, dual BiLSTM layers, and CTC decoder achieved 72.6% character accuracy with vowels (74.2%) exceeding consonants (72.3%) through implicit boundary learning. 50-fold augmentation addressed dataset limitations while confusion matrix analysis revealed degradation-tier-specific error patterns.

www.ingramcontent.com/pod-product-compliance
Lightning Source LLC
LaVergne TN
LVHW010721061126
851857LV00014B/1294
* 9 7 9 8 1 8 2 7 2 4 6 7 8 *